Pilgrims from the Sun

WEST INDIAN MIGRATION TO AMERICA

Twayne's Immigrant Heritage of America Series

Thomas J. Archdeacon, General Editor

Pilgrims from the Sun

WEST INDIAN MIGRATION TO AMERICA

Ransford W. Palmer

TWAYNE PUBLISHERS
An Imprint of Simon & Schuster Macmillan
New York

Prentice Hall International
London Mexico City New Delhi Singapore Sydney Toronto

Pilgrims from the Sun: West Indian Migration to America
Ransford W. Palmer

Copyright © 1995 by Ransford W. Palmer

Twayne Publishers
An Imprint of Simon & Schuster Macmillan
866 Third Avenue
New York, New York 10022

Library of Congress Cataloging-in-Publication Data

Palmer, Ransford W.
Pilgrims from the sun : West Indian migration to America
p. cm.—(Twayne's immigrant heritage of America series)
Includes bibliographical references and index.
ISBN 0-8057-8431-4.—ISBN 0-8057-4546-7 (pbk.)
1. West Indian Americans—Economic conditions. 2. West Indians—United
States—Economic conditions. 3. West Indies, British—Emigration and immi-
gration. I. Title. II. Series.
E184.W54P35 1995
330.973'0089'969729—dc20   94-36254
                                                                 CIP

The paper used in this publication meets the minimum requirements of
American National Standard for Information Sciences—Permanence of Paper
for Printed Library Materials, ANSI Z39.48-1984. (∞) ™

10 9 8 7 6 5 4 3 2 1 (hc.)
10 9 8 7 6 5 4 3 2 1 (pbk.)

Printed in the United States of America.

In Memory of
My Mother and Father

Contents

Tables

Preface

The focus of this volume is the migration of people from the English-speaking Caribbean to the United States. Because migration is an integral part of the history of Caribbean peoples, chapter 1 begins with an overview of migration between emancipation in 1838 and World War II. After the abolition of slavery, the declining sugar economies of the British Caribbean were unable to provide a livelihood for large numbers of freed slaves. As a consequence, many of them migrated to Panama, Costa Rica, and Cuba, where American investments in the Panama canal and in railroads created a demand for unskilled workers. When these projects ended in the early decades of the twentieth century, the demand for foreign workers dried up and most of those who were abroad were repatriated. The deterioration of economic conditions and rising unemployment in the British Caribbean fueled social and political upheavals across the region in the late 1930s. During World War II many West Indians were recruited to work in agriculture and in nondefense industries. Others went to Britain to serve in the armed forces.

Chapter 2 examines the massive post–World War II migration of Caribbean people. This began with the movement to Britain in the 1950s, which came to an end in 1962 when Britain enacted legislation to restrict it. The chapter then examines the shift of the migration flow from Britain to the United States after 1962 when the era of political independence began.

Chapter 3 focuses on the settlement of the immigrants in the United States, with particular emphasis on New York City, where the great majority of them live. It paints a picture of the contemporary West Indian community against the historical background of West Indians who have played prominent roles in the social, economic, and political life of New York from the early part of this century. Chapter 4 analyzes the employment characteristics and economic status of the immigrants, comparing their incomes with those of white and black Americans. The chapter also assesses the progress of West Indians by comparing them with one other immigrant group—Filipinos. In this comparison, the significance of education for group advancement is explored. Finally, the chapter examines the demographic and economic environment at a particular destination—King's County, New York—which has the highest concentration of West Indians in the United States.

Chapter 5 discusses the temporary movement of people from the Caribbean to the United States, paying special attention to the seasonal migration of farm workers to southern Florida and to the growth of the number of temporary visitors for pleasure and for business. The chapter also looks at the flow of students to the United States and the problem of illegal migration.

Chapter 6 provides an overall assessment of the gains from migration, with special emphasis on the gains to the immigrants in terms of upward occupational mobility and gains to the countries of origin in the form of immigrant remittances.

The relationship between migration, employment, and trade is treated at some length in chapter 7. The discussion explores the impact of trade on migration as well as the impact of migration on trade. Chapter 8 reviews the pattern of past migration, including return migration, and constructs a theory that explains contemporary migration as circular. The chapter concludes with the argument that only accelerated growth that reduces the disparity in living standards between the Caribbean and the United States can stem the flow of immigrants.

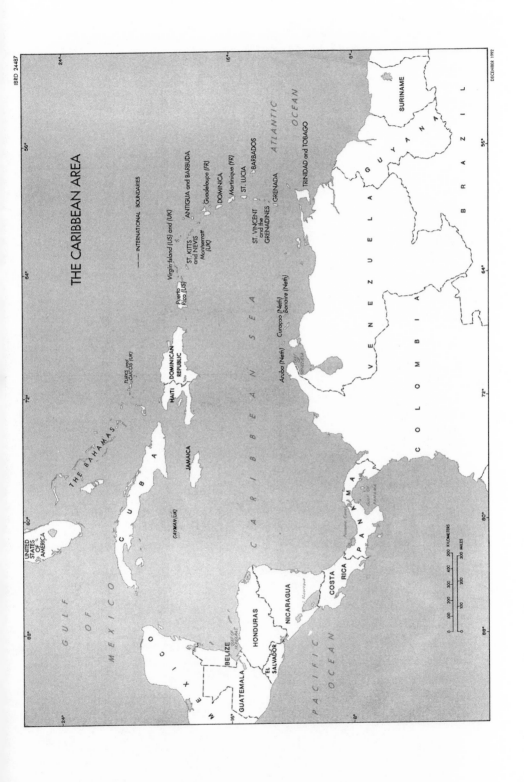

THE CARIBBEAN AREA

one

Post-Emancipation Migration

L arge-scale migration from the British West Indies can be said to begin in the latter half of the nineteenth century. Prior to that time the slave trade brought large numbers of Africans from West Africa (primarily from what is now known as Ghana) to the islands to work in the sugar cane fields. Throughout the history of slavery, the natural increase in the population was offset by the death of slaves from diseases and harsh living conditions. The slave population of the islands grew only by the importation of additional slaves.

The combination of slave labor and the monopoly which the West Indian planters enjoyed in the British sugar market made the British Caribbean sugar industry extremely profitable in the eighteenth century. It also made the Caribbean colonies more important to Britain than its New England colonies. Because of its profitability, sugar came to dominate the island economies, pushing traditional export crops such as cotton and tobacco into insignificance. As long as they maintained their monopoly and had access to free labor, the planters had no incentive to modernize production methods.

The Fall of Sugar

The British West Indies sugar estates produced muscovado sugar through a process of draining off the liquid molasses from sugar crystals. The invention of the centrifuge in 1837 encouraged the continued production of muscovado sugar by shortening considerably the time needed for the extraction process. The West Indies muscovado estates, however, were inefficient. They relied on an inferior kind of mill for crushing the cane. According to R. W. Beachey, "the most prominent characteristics of the muscovado sugar industry were wastefulness and slovenliness" (Beachey 1957, 61). As a result, although sugar cane contains about 87 percent of its weight in juice, the muscovado estates were only able to extract 50–60 percent, with the rest going to waste. The muscovado estates were much less productive than those in British Guiana (now Guyana) and Trinidad, where mills with four rollers instead of three were used for crushing cane (Beachey 1957, 62). The gap became even greater when these two colonies combined the centrifuge with the vacuum pan process. The vacuum pan, in contrast to the open pan, lowers the temperature at which the boiling of the cane juice takes place, thereby enabling speedy evaporation and a reduction of the amount of molasses produced (Beachey 1957, 68). The big advantage of the muscovado estates was the rich molasses by-product, from which rum was made. As sugar prices fell in the latter half of the nineteenth century, rum exports gained in importance (Beachey 1957, 72–80).

The fall of sugar in the British Caribbean from its eighteenth-century dominance is attributed to the abolition of slavery and the loss of monopoly power by the planters. The abolition of the slave trade in 1808 and slavery in 1838 undermined the competitive position of the West Indian sugar industry. It now had to compete not only with better capitalized producers in Cuba and elsewhere but also with countries where slavery had not yet been abolished.

Another major blow befell the industry in 1846 when the British government passed the Sugar Duties Act, which provided for a reduction in the tariff on sugar until the tariff on sugar from all sources was equalized by 1854. West Indian planters found themselves in direct competition with more efficient producers. Moreover, a sharp increase in the world sugar supply from both cane and beet sources further eroded the West Indian position. The increased cane sugar production came from major non-British Caribbean producers, such as Cuba and Brazil, and from Louisiana, where greater investment in production modernization had taken place, where slavery had not yet been abolished, and where the soil had not yet been overworked as in the Caribbean. In Europe, beet sugar production had made substantial gains without the use of slave labor.

The increase in world sugar production depressed sugar prices at a time when the industrial revolution in Britain was gaining momentum, a development that spelled the end of mercantilism and ushered in an era of free trade. The relative decline of British West Indian sugar production continued through the nineteenth century, falling from 16 percent of the world cane sugar production in 1839–43 to 5 percent in 1899–1903. Over that same period its share of total world production (including beet sugar) fell from 15 percent to 2 percent (Fraser 1990, 20).

During the second half of the nineteenth century the Crown foreclosed on many sugar estates in Jamaica for nonpayment of quit-rent. Beachey writes, "Patents of land granted by the Crown, in the early years of the colony, were made, subject to the payment of annual quit-rent by grantees." These payments had not been punctual, and virtually ceased after emancipation. The forfeiture of thousands of acres by the Crown increased the available acreage on which laborers could settle and grow provisions (Beachey 1957, 124).

In the wake of the abolition of slavery in the British Caribbean, large numbers of workers left the sugar plantations. Those who had accumulated savings from the Sunday market sale of root crops they were allowed to cultivate as slaves were able to acquire property from the Crown, which had foreclosed on owners of marginal plantations that were experiencing difficulties. In the smaller colonies, these peasant holdings were usually adjacent to the sugar estates, but in Jamaica many peasants settled in the hinterland.

Planters found it increasingly difficult to attract freed workers to toil on their estates. Former slaves and their descendants unhappily remembered the harsh conditions of the past and were unwilling to accept the meager wages being offered. Planters assumed that "the negro would work only sufficiently to obtain the necessaries of life" and that "if wages were lowered, the negro would work harder to attain the bare minimum necessary for the hand-to-mouth existence he desired" (Beachey 1957, 106). Thus, to the planter, to raise wages above the subsistence minimum would have no effect on the labor supply. Clearly, this was a misperception on the part of the planters because laborers were eager to migrate to neighboring countries where the wage rates were higher.

The unwillingness of the freed slaves to work for low plantation wages and the planters' loss of control over the workers created an artificial shortage of labor. In response, the planters induced the colonial government to import indentured workers from India. Most of the Indians went to Trinidad and Tobago and British Guiana, and only a small number went to Barbados and Jamaica. Beachey reports that "the system of coolie [cheap labor from Asia, particularly Indians] organization was functioning best in the colonies of Trinidad and British Guiana. By 1870, 44,825 coolies had entered British Guiana and all of the 128 sugar estates relied on coolies for their labour force" (Beachey 1957, 99). The greatest immigration of indentured workers in the British West Indies was to Trinidad where there were 110,000 by 1900 (Beachey 1957, 102, 104). The cost of this immigration was borne largely by the colonial governments, a situation that constituted a bounty to the planters. Although the immigration of indentured workers to Jamaica was nowhere as large as in Trinidad and British Guiana, it was nevertheless "a burden on the revenues of the colony." By 1877, the governor of Jamaica reported that the immigration fund was insolvent with an outstanding debt of £140,000 (Beachey 1957, 107).

Despite this new wave of cheap labor, the sugar industry never fully recovered from the precipitous decline in prices in 1846. And because the industry dominated the island economies, its decline created severe hardship for both sugar workers and peasant farmers. Since the crops the peasant farmers produced were sold to the sugar workers, a decline in the fortunes of sugar also meant a decline in the market for peasant crops. Aggravating the situation was the Civil War in America in the first half of the 1860s, which increased the price of such imported staples as saltfish and grain. All of these events occurred against the background of a post-emancipation population that was rapidly rising owing to falling death rates and rising birth rates. Between 1844 and 1911, the population of Jamaica more than doubled, growing from 377,433 to 831,383 (Fraser 1990, 24). Together, these developments constituted the major push force behind the rise of post-emancipation emigration.

The major pull force abroad was the huge foreign investment, primarily American, in infrastructural projects such as the canal in Panama and railroads in Central America and Cuba. These investments accelerated the growth of export agriculture in those countries and, in the process, generated a considerable increase in the demand for unskilled workers from the British West Indies.

Migration to Caribbean and Central American Countries

Post-emancipation migration falls into two main phases. The first phase occurred between 1835 and 1885 after slavery was abolished in the British West Indies and before it disappeared in the Hispanic Caribbean and in America.

Migration during this period was primarily to other British West Indian colonies. The second phase was from 1885 to 1920, when migration was primarily to Central America and the Hispanic Caribbean. There was little or no migration to the United States.

The movement to other parts of the British West Indies was largely to Trinidad and Tobago and British Guiana where there had been considerable investment in plant modernization in the sugar industry. According to Marshall, Trinidadian and Guianese planters had active recruitment programs and paid wage rates that were double those in other islands. Trinidadian planters also adopted a bounty system in which captains of sailing vessels were paid for each laborer they imported (Marshall 1987, 17).

The migration to Trinidad took place despite the largest population of indentured labor in the West Indies. Planters believed that former slaves and their descendants were better suited for field tasks such as trenching and cane cutting and for some of the principal mill tasks such as boiling (Beachey 1957, 100). Furthermore, many indentured workers opted for private cultivation on available Crown lands after their initial five-year indenture contract expired, despite a bounty offered by planters for reindenturing (Beachey 1957, 101).

Although migration in this first phase was primarily to other British West Indian colonies, in the 1850s, West Indians traveled to Panama to build the railway connecting the Atlantic and Pacific Oceans. A decade later, they helped to build railways in Costa Rica and Mexico (Fraser 1990, 23).

In the second migration phase to Central America and the Hispanic Caribbean, Gisela Eisner identifies three waves apart from the brief exodus to Panama in 1853 and 1854 to build the railway. The first and second waves went to Panama and Costa Rica during the 1880s and after the turn of the century, and the third wave went to Cuba between 1916 and 1920 (Eisner 1961, 148). Between 1904 and 1914, large numbers of West Indians were recruited by Americans to work on the Panama canal. Most of these migrants were from Jamaica, but many were from Barbados. According to Bonham Richardson, "an estimated 45,000 black Barbadians emigrated to Panama and the Canal Zone during the first two decades of the twentieth century" (Richardson 1985, 143). The planting of bananas in Costa Rica also attracted many West Indians. Eisner estimates that by 1911–12, 60,000 Jamaicans were in Central America. In the decade after the completion of the Panama canal, Cuba became the major destination for West Indian migrants. Between 1913 and 1924, according to Eric Williams, "Cuba received 217,000 labourers from Haiti, Jamaica and Puerto Rico; in the single year 1920, as many as 63,000 from Haiti and Jamaica" (Williams 1970, 438). This migration wave was triggered by the post–World War I boom in the price of sugar and the inability of the West Indian economies to employ their rapidly increasing labor force. Fraser maintains that while there were noneconomic reasons for post-emancipation migration, such as the "search for independence from the domination exercised by plantation owners," the economic motivation in the form of wage differential was foremost (Fraser 1990, 25).

At a time when political enfranchisement required property ownership, migration offered an opportunity to accumulate savings to buy property. Hence, the ownership of a house, a small farm, or a small business became an overriding objective for most immigrants. The money they brought back with them plus that which they remitted while abroad had a significant impact on the local economy. Between 1906 and 1915, Barbadian migrants to the Canal Zone remitted and brought back with them an estimated total of £650,000 ($3.25 million) (Richardson 1985, 144, 152). Richardson relates the story of the Barbadian immigrants to Panama: "The building of a new chattel house for his mother or his wife—or, for a bachelor, house construction to enhance his marriage prospects—was perhaps the first real goal of a returned Barbadian from the Canal Zone . . . After his home was built, however, the desire to earn the money necessary to purchase the land on which it stood often pushed a Barbadian veteran of Panama back again to Central America or on to a new external labor destination" (Richardson 1985, 168). His next destination was usually determined by the location of foreign capital investment.

Migration to Panama, Costa Rica, and Cuba was seasonal in character. Workers returned home after their contracts expired. Despite the temporary nature of the migration, small permanent settlements were created in some countries, especially in Panama. According to Eisener, the French Panama canal project attracted as many as 23,401 Jamaicans in 1883. And when the project failed in 1889, more than 6,000 were left in Panama after the Jamaican government took steps to repatriate those who were in hardship (Eisner 1961, 148).

Several events converged in the 1920s to restrict West Indian migration to Central America and Cuba: the fall of sugar prices in the depression of 1921; the devastation of the banana crop by Panama disease; and the completion of canal and railroad projects. The fall of sugar prices created widespread unemployment among the sugar workers of Cuba, and the conditions of immigrant workers were particularly difficult. Most of the West Indian immigrants elected to stay in Cuba despite the hardship, hoping that things would turn around. But in the 1930s their discontent led to violence and they were forcibly repatriated (Marshall 1987, 22). In 1935, the return of 12,000 families to Jamaica from Cuba and Panama alone intensified the unemployment problem (Kaplan 1976, 79). The outbreak of Panama disease in Costa Rican bananas and the completion of the Panama canal and the railroad projects in Central America drastically reduced the demand for West Indian workers.

The cessation of immigration and the repatriation of workers who had been earning higher wages abroad aggravated an already tense social and economic situation in the West Indies. In 1938, the minimum wage of a field laborer in the Cuban sugar industry was 80 cents a day, compared with 48–60 cents in Jamaica, 30 cents in Barbados and St. Lucia, 30–48 cents in Grenada, and 28 cents in St. Vincent (Williams 1970, 444). Williams writes that "nearly half the wage-earning population in Jamaica obtained only intermittent employment, and both government and private employers adopted the policy of 'rotational employment'—a worker worked for a fortnight and then was discharged to make way for another" (Williams 1970, 446). As unemployment rose and living conditions deteriorated, many foreign-owned industries were declaring high profits. Eric Williams notes that "while the oil companies [in Trinidad] declared dividends of 45 and 30 percent, and while profits for 1935–36 were four times the wages bill," unskilled workers were being paid an average wage of 72 cents a day (Williams 1970, 443).

The cessation of migration to Panama and Central America, the depression of 1921, and the lingering impact of a series of natural disasters, including the

1907 earthquake, which devastated Kingston and Port Royal in Jamaica, made life difficult for the people of the British Caribbean. An American traveler to Jamaica in 1920 was dismayed by what he saw in Kingston:

> Kingston is the most disappointing town in the West Indies. With the exception of a few bright yellow public buildings and a scattered block or two of new business houses, it is a negro slum, spreading for miles over a dusty plain. Scarcely a street has even the pretense of a pavement; the few sidewalks that exist are blocked by stairways, posts, and the trash of a disorderly population or degenerates every few yards in stretches of loose stones and earth. The only building worth crossing the street to see is that domed structure sighted from the bay, the Catholic cathedral. To be sure, the earthquake [of 1907] wrought great havoc, but that was thirteen years ago, time enough surely in which to have made a much faster advance toward recovery (Frank 1970, 404).

One hundred years after emancipation, discontent throughout the West Indies culminated in the 1938 uprising in Jamaica, when rioting by sugar workers at Frome Sugar estates at the western end of the island touched off massive riots by dock workers in Kingston. Out of these disturbances emerged two leaders— Alexander Bustamante and Norman Manley—who were to lead Jamaica into political independence 24 years later. In response to the disturbances, the British government dispatched a royal commission headed by Lord Moyne to investigate the social and economic conditions in the colonies. The commission held extensive hearings in Jamaica and "received written and oral testimony from every conceivable organization in the island." The final draft of the report was considered such "a severe indictment of the colonial system in the West Indies that its publication was postponed until the end of World War II" (Kaplan 1976, 82).

Recommendations released in 1940 led the British government to pass the Colonial Development and Welfare Act. The act, administered by the Colonial Development and Welfare Organization, provided £1 million a year for 20 years to finance education and social welfare throughout the British West Indies. But as important as this money was, John Mordecai, secretary-general of the West Indies Regional Economic Committee, saw the major significance of the act in its treatment of the West Indies as a unit with common problems, a treatment that was to lay the groundwork for a West Indian Federation (Mordecai 1968, 31).

Migration to the United States

Migration to the United States began in the early part of the twentieth century and was facilitated by the development of the banana industry by the United Fruit Company. While banana growing gave new life to the small farmer because the crop could be grown on terrain unsuitable for sugar cane, it also brought the banana boat, which signaled the development of a tourist industry. The banana boats also brought passengers and marked the beginning of regular steamship travel between the Caribbean and the Atlantic ports of the United States, especially New York. The development of passenger travel by ship facilitated migration to New York.

In the 1920s, the United States entered a period of restrictive immigration policies toward Eastern Hemisphere countries. The Quota Act of 1921 limited the annual number of entrants of each admissible nationality to 3 percent of the foreign-born of that nationality as recorded in the U.S. Census of 1910. In doing so, the act favored Northern and Western Europeans, who were already present in large numbers in America. These groups (including those from the British Isles) received 82 percent of the total annual quota (Bernard 1982, 98). The trend toward immigration restriction continued with the Immigration Act of 1924. Not only did it lower the annual quota for each nation, it introduced visas that allowed American consular officers to limit the number of immigrants and to select those most likely to assimilate into American society by screening them in their home countries. The law reaffirmed the exclusion of Chinese and banned many other Asians, including Japanese, who were declared racially ineligible (Bernard 1982, 97). As William Bernard puts it, "the national origins system was designed to prevent further changes in the ethnic composition of American society that might come from a new infusion of immigrants" (Bernard 1982, 98).

Migration from Western Hemisphere countries remained unrestricted. West Indian immigrants were able to enter the United States under the umbrella of the British quota. Aside from those West Indians who entered directly from the colonies, there were others who came from Panama and Costa Rica, where they had settled after construction of the Panama canal and the Costa Rican railroad. Pastor points out that the resulting reduction in the number of immigrants from Southern and Eastern Europe "permitted increases in immigration from Mexico and the West Indies. Immigration from the Caribbean averaged about 1,000 per year from 1899 to 1904. From then till 1923 it increased and averaged 3–7 thousand per year. It expanded to 10,630 in 1924. . . . Congress handled the perceived problem associated with the dramatic increase in immigrants from the British West Indies by assigning them the quotas of their mother countries" (Pastor 1987, 245). This Pastor attributed to racism, since other Western Hemisphere countries were permitted unlimited entry.

Despite the fact that West Indians could migrate to the United States under a large British quota, the number of immigrants fell sharply following the passage of the Immigration Act of 1924, from 10,000 in 1924 to only 308 in 1925. It averaged 617 persons a year from then through 1932 (Pastor 1987, 247).

The decline of West Indian migration to America must also be seen against the overall cessation of mass migration in the late 1920s owing to the onset of the Great Depression. According to Vernon Briggs, "in 1933, only 23,068 persons migrated to the United States; the number had not been that low since 1929. Even the minimal quotas assigned to the countries of eastern and southern Europe had not been met in the early 1930s. It is believed that in 1933, more people emigrated than immigrated. Mass unemployment had replaced mass immigration as the labor market issue of the times. With a general labor surplus, there was no need for immigrant workers of any skill capability" (Briggs 1992, 71).

Although poverty in the Caribbean was the main push factor behind West Indian emigration, Calvin Holder notes that the emigrants included "clerks in private enterprise and junior civil servants who were comparatively well paid and lived measurably well, some of them with servants of their own" (Holder 1987, 11). Holder argues that the prospects for people in those positions were limited at home and that the stories they heard from tourists and emigrants raised their expectations about what New York City had to offer as a place in which a professional career could be pursued. The immigrants preferred New York City to Florida by a wide margin (Holder 1987, 14). New York was seen as being more cosmopolitan and holding greater economic opportunities than the agriculture and tourist economy of Florida. But equally important, the immigrants perceived New York to be more racially hospitable than Florida or any other part of the country. Holder writes that "they were appalled by the vicious forms of physical abuse to which blacks were subjected in [Florida], such as were unheard of in the West Indies" (Holder 1987, 16).

World War II brought a new role for the United States in the Caribbean as a protector of the region from possible German attack. Through lend-lease arrangements with Britain, the United States acquired 90-year base rights in Jamaica and in other islands in 1940. Under the aegis of the Anglo-American Caribbean Commission established in 1942, West Indian workers were recruited during the war to replace American workers in agriculture and nondefense industries.

In sum, the history of Caribbean migration up to World War II was essentially a history of the flight from the legacy of slavery. Colonial capitalism was unprepared to provide the region's freed labor force with a decent livelihood. Before emancipation, colonial capitalism depended on free labor, and after emancipation, cheap labor. After emancipation it took large American investment in modern agricultural and transportation projects in Central America and Cuba to provide the large number of unskilled workers from the British West Indies with jobs. Although the availability of these workers kept wage rates low, wages were nevertheless higher than in their own countries. Unable to create jobs at home, the British colonial governments acted as suppliers of labor as they encouraged and facilitated the movement. The fact is that the British colonies, having been accustomed to involuntary full employment under slavery, were completely unable or unwilling to restructure their economies fully to employ freed labor. Instead, they came to depend on economic growth abroad to reduce their high rates of domestic unemployment.

two

Post–World War II Caribbean Migration

D uring World War II many West Indians were recruited to work in agriculture and in nondefense industries in America. Many others went to Britain to join the armed forces. In the West Indies, where consumption depended heavily on imported goods, economic conditions during the war were defined by a persistent shortage of consumer goods. The war restricted shipping and therefore the exports on which a large segment of the labor force depended. Against this background, the farm workers who returned from America with money and goods were regarded by most people as having achieved an enviable economic status. They also returned with stories of racism and economic opportunities in America. Many farm workers who skipped their contract to take advantage of these economic opportunities later managed to become permanent residents.

As bad as conditions in the West Indies were during the war, they were at least partially alleviated by the recruitment of farm workers and by the flow of men to Britain to join the armed forces. When the war ended, these avenues of work virtually came to an end, causing a sharp rise in the unemployment rate. After the war, the unemployment rate in Jamaica rose to an estimated 30 percent of the labor force. In the building industry, which accounted for roughly 14 percent of the labor force, unemployment was as high as 40 percent (Palmer 1968, 3). Between 1943 and 1950, the Jamaican labor force grew at an average annual rate of 4 percent while real gross domestic product (GDP) grew at only 2.5 percent (Palmer 1968, 4). Many were ready to seek out economic opportunities abroad to improve their condition, just as their fathers did when they migrated to Central America and other parts of the Caribbean in the latter part of the nineteenth century.

To understand the direction and magnitude of post-war Caribbean migration it is important to understand the role of immigration laws in the major receiving countries. If migration is an escape valve, then the immigration laws in the receiving countries are the spigots that control the direction and volume of the migration flow. When a national law tightens the spigot, closing off the flow of immigrants, a reservoir of potential immigrants builds up, waiting to be released in some other direction by the change of another country's laws. Nations tighten or loosen the immigration spigot depending on their domestic social and economic priorities. The shortage of labor during the economic boom of the United

States in the 1960s and the civil rights movement of that time, for example, were major factors behind the liberalization of U.S. immigration policy in 1965. Under the McCarran-Walter Act of 1952, U.S. immigration policy favored immigrants from Europe, a policy that was incompatible with the 1964 Civil Rights Act banning racial discrimination at home. The McCarran-Walter Act forbid West Indians to migrate under the British limit and imposed a quota of 100 visas on the colonial dependencies of Europe. This severely restricted immigration from the black English-speaking Caribbean countries. There were no such restrictions on migration to Britain.

Migration to Great Britain: End of the War to 1962

As citizens of the United Kingdom, West Indians migrated to Britain with the same facility that Puerto Ricans migrated to the United States after the war. While population growth combined with the desperate post-war economic conditions of these colonies pushed people toward the mother country, the shortage of unskilled labor in Britain pulled them in.

The discovery of bauxite in Jamaica led to a substantial inflow of foreign capital after the war. But this did not quell the desire on the part of many to migrate. The discovery of bauxite drove up land prices considerably, and many peasant farmers who had inherited lands from their freed slave ancestors sold out to the bauxite companies to finance their trip to Britain. One of the ironies of the time is that large-scale migration to Britain coincided with the large-scale inflow of capital investment into the bauxite industry. This investment did not create much employment because of the capital intensive nature of bauxite mining. It provided high wage jobs for a relatively small group of skilled workers.

The first post-war contingent of 492 Jamaicans arrived in Britain on 22 June 1948 on the SS *Empire Windrush*. Between 1953 and 1962, there was a net migration of 163,069 Jamaicans to Britain (Smith 1981, 154). More than half of this migration occurred in the three years between 1960 and 1962, when it was feared that Britain would soon terminate the flow. In 1961, the prime minister of Jamaica, Norman Manley, and the leader of the opposition, Alexander Bustamante, protested the impending immigration controls being discussed in Britain (Smith 1981, 158). The position of West Indian governments on the issue was captured by the region's leading demographer, George Roberts: "It seems therefore that immigration to the United Kingdom constituting a powerful curb on population growth has come to be accepted by the West Indian Governments, who, having realized its immediate advantages, are prepared to do everything within their power to maintain it" (Roberts 1962, 349).

The protests of the Jamaican government were of no avail. In 1962, Britain passed the Commonwealth Immigrants Act, which effectively terminated immigration for work. The immigration of relatives and dependents continued for several years after, trailing off from 9,974 in 1964 to 1,620 in 1972 (Smith 1972, 163). As it was directed against nonwhite Commonwealth immigrants and not Irish immigrants, the Commonwealth Immigrants Act was racially discriminatory. Furthermore, "the Immigration Act of 1971, the product of the Tory government of Edward Heath, employed the transparent device of a grandfather clause to enable white Commonwealth residents to evade its [the 1962 Act] controls. Under this law persons who had a parent or a grandparent born in the U.K. are considered partials and are granted free entry" (Freeman 1990, 188).

The migration of West Indians to Britain transformed them into a racial minority in a white society and exposed them to racial hostility for which their previous experience had not prepared them. West Indian soldiers who had served in Britain during the war had brought back mostly news about economic opportunities (Thompson 1990, 39–70). Thompson writes that "it is almost inconceivable that these returning soldiers would not have informed people about their adverse experiences in England. Whether those listening would have been able to interpret the meaning, however, was a different matter, especially when unlike black Americans, the majority of Afro-Caribbean peoples had never experienced overt white racism, either as rural workers or in a modern urban/industrial context" (Thompson 1990, 44–45). Yet so great was the psychological capital they had invested in their British citizenship that it was inconceivable to them that they would not be well received under the revered Union Jack. In the past they had often left the "security" of the Union Jack to earn American dollars elsewhere in the Caribbean. Now they were moving in great numbers to the very heart of the empire that their forbears had slaved to enrich only to discover that their citizenship was second class.

Contemporary Migration to the United States

As table 2.1 shows, there was a surge of migration from the English-speaking Caribbean countries to the United States in the 1960s. Several factors accounted for this: the achievement of political independence from Great Britain, begin-

Table 2.1

Migration from the Caribbean to the United States by Country or Region of Birth, 1925–1989

Years	Caribbean	Br. W. Indies	Cuba	Dom. Rep.	Haiti	Jamaica[a]	Trinidad and Tobago[a]	Barbados[a]	Guyana[a]
1925–30	20,444	5,195	13,085	1,162	351	—	—	—	614
1931–40	10,129	3,953	4,768	1,075	156	—	—	—	293
1941–50	41,095	15,801	18,382	4,916	766	—	—	—	1,005
1951–60	122,867	8,091[b]	78,330	9,755	4,713	8,659[c]	1,074[c]	1,845[c]	1,593
1961–70	519,595	—	256,769	94,116	37,537	71,011	24,516	9,304	6,999
1971–80	759,829	—	276,788	148,016	58,705	141,995	61,776	20,948	47,531
1981–89	777,352	—	148,612	209,608	119,839	188,792	32,793	15,737	84,012

Source: Statistical Division, U.S. Immigration and Naturalization Service, Washington, D.C.
[a]Data for 1925–30, 1931–40, and 1941–50 included in British West Indies.
[b]Includes years 1951 to 1958. After this period, data were compiled only for individual countries.
[c]Includes years 1952 to 1960.

ning in 1962; the termination of migration to Great Britain by the 1962 British immigration law; and vigorous economic growth in the United States.

Jamaica and Trinidad and Tobago gained their political independence in 1962, followed by Barbados and Guyana in 1966 and the smaller eastern Caribbean islands over the next two decades. As sovereign nations, these countries benefitted from the nonquota immigration status accorded to Western Hemisphere nations up to 1 July 1968 when the Immigration and Nationality Act of 1965 came into effect. The termination of large-scale migration to Britain had created a large pool of potential emigrants who wanted to improve their economic condition. They were also abetted by vigorous economic growth, which propelled the United States toward full employment for the first time since World War II, and by their uncertainty about the economic viability of their small Caribbean economies. Ironically, it took political independence to open a new escape valve for them.

The 1965 Immigration and Nationality Act imposed a quota for the first time on immigration from the Western Hemisphere: an annual maximum of 120,000. The act did not impose a system of preferences and a quota for individual countries. In 1976, however, amendments to the act applied the seven-category preference system to the Western Hemisphere nations as a way of regulating the flow of immigrants under the 120,000 ceiling. A ceiling of 20,000 was imposed on each country for the first time, excluding close relatives of U.S. citizens. This means that immigration in any one year from a particular Western Hemisphere country could exceed 20,000. Between 1925 and 1989, 2.25 million people migrated from the Caribbean to the United States. (See table 2.1.) This is roughly equal to the entire population of Jamaica. Ninety-one percent of this movement occurred after 1961, with Cubans accounting for the largest share at 35 percent. On the surface, the migration of Cubans appeared to be a political movement, but many were simply escaping the harsh economic conditions of communist Cuba. While U.S. immigration authorities treated the Cubans as political refugees, the rest of the immigrants from the Caribbean were regarded as economic immigrants who left their countries voluntarily to seek a better life in the United States. The largest stream of economic immigrants have come from the Dominican Republic, Jamaica, Haiti, and Guyana. Together they accounted for 67 percent of all Caribbean immigrants in the 1980s. The U.S. distinction between an economic immigrant and a political refugee is determined by whether or not one is fleeing political oppression in a communist country. But political oppression can be just as real in a noncommunist country. The examples of Haiti and Guyana illustrate this quite well. Political repression in both countries has stimulated an exodus of people to the United States, but the United States has classified only a handful of them as political refugees. Many people in Guyana, especially among the Indo-Guyanese community, feel that the social and political repression wrought by the dictatorship of the late Forbes Burnham made migration their only option. Yet it is difficult to separate the political from the economic motive when economic conditions at home are deteriorating. An argument can be made that people, seeing a reduction of their lifetime earnings under a particular political regime, will choose to migrate to a country where those earnings and the condition of work might be enhanced. In this regard, their motive is economic even if it may have been brought about by a repressive political regime.

Since 1961, the four major English-speaking Caribbean countries—Jamaica, Trinidad and Tobago, Barbados, and Guyana—have supplied one-third of all Caribbean immigrants to the United States. By far the largest number from this group has come from Jamaica. The magnitude of this migration is underscored when it is calculated as a percentage of their current populations: 18 percent for Barbados, 17 percent for Jamaica, 14 percent for Guyana, and 10 percent for Trinidad and Tobago.

An examination of the occupational distribution of the immigrants from the three largest non-Cuban Caribbean suppliers—the Dominican Republic, Jamaica, and Haiti—shows some important differences in the nature of the movement. (See table 2.2.) On average, immigrants from Jamaica had the largest shares of workers at both ends of the occupational spectrum—professionals at one end and service workers at the other—while immigrants from the Dominican Republic had the smallest share of professionals. In general, the occupational distribution of migration from these countries has been heavily skewed toward service and factory workers. Most of those classified as service workers are private household workers. Demand for these workers began to accelerate in the 1960s when large numbers of American women entered the full-employment U.S. economy. Chapter 4 will discuss this further.

The Impact of Migration on the Sending Countries

In 1962, when the British legislated a virtual end to West Indian migration to their country, the West Indies were left with virtually no population escape valve. The point system introduced by Canada in 1962 favored skilled workers from the Caribbean, but the Canadian quota was too small to make much difference.

Table 2.2

Percentage Distribution of the Occupations of Immigrants from Jamaica, the Dominican Republic, and Haiti, 1962–1988

Occupation	Jamaica	Dom. Rep.	Haiti
Prof. and tech. workers	14.3	7.3	13.3
Exec., admin., and managerial	4.8	5.0	2.9
Sales	2.4	2.4	1.2
Admin. support	13.9	7.0	8.8
Precision prod., craft, and repair	16.1	14.2	16.9
Operators, fabricators, and laborers	13.3	30.1	29.8
Farming, forestry, and fishing	3.3	7.2	2.5
Service workers	31.6	26.6	24.1

Source: Statistical Division, U.S. Immigration and Naturalization Service, Washington, D.C.

Between 1963 and 1966, the newly politically independent former British colonies came face-to-face with their population problem. Migration from Jamaica to the United States during this period represented less than 4 percent of the net increase in the population. For Trinidad and Tobago, Barbados, and Guyana, the percentages were 2.1, 9.4, and 1.5, respectively. Over the succeeding four years, 1967 to 1970, there was a surge of migration as emigrants began to take advantage of the access that their newly acquired independent status accorded them. Migration as a percentage of the net increase in population rose sharply to 29.3 for Jamaica, 28.3 for Trinidad and Tobago, 53.2 for Barbados, and 7.1 for Guyana. These percentages have remained high since. It follows, therefore, that during the period when West Indians were locked in, the acceleration of population growth put more pressure on the countries' limited productive capacity. From 1963 to 1966 their populations thus increased as follows: 7.4 percent for Jamaica, 7.6 percent for Trinidad and Tobago, .05 percent for Barbados, and 7.4 percent for Guyana. From 1967 to 1970, when migration surged, the population increase was quite a bit lower for Jamaica (3.8 percent), Trinidad and Tobago (1.6 percent), and Guyana (6.6 percent), but remained stable for Barbados (.05 percent) (Palmer 1979). It is clear that the major beneficiaries of this new opportunity to migrate were Jamaica and Trinidad and Tobago.

Because Jamaica has the largest population of all the English-speaking Caribbean countries, it is used to illustrate the economic impact of the closing and opening of the population escape valve. During the period when the valve was closed, Jamaica's GDP grew by 26 percent, well over three times the 7.4 percent increase in its population. In 1967–70, when there was a surge of emigration, the GDP increased by 34.8 percent, representing growth almost 10 times the size of the 3.8 percent increase in population. The implication is that per capita GDP grew much faster in the latter period than in the former.

Clearly, the growth in per capita GDP, and by implication the standard of living, cannot be attributed solely to emigration. Other factors were at work, such as the increased inflow of foreign capital and the growth of exports. These two factors are directly related to the vigorous growth of the U.S. economy at the time. Corporate profits were high and American multinational firms were spreading their wings abroad. This helped to increase net capital movements into Jamaica by 354 percent and exports by 10.6 percent over the 1963–66 period. In the years 1967–70, exports grew even faster (43 percent), while the growth in capital inflow continued to be impressive (229 percent). Thus as migration reduced the rate of population growth and therefore the rate of increase in the labor force, the country's stock of capital was augmented significantly by foreign capital. The net effect is a larger ratio of capital to labor, a situation that augurs well for greater labor productivity.

Yet the impact of emigration on Jamaica was not viewed by the government as entirely positive, especially after 1970. In a broadcast to the Jamaican people on 5 January 1977, Prime Minister Michael Manley was clearly troubled by the fact that "many business enterprises were closed because some people were afraid to continue living here. Many professionals were persuaded to leave Jamaica for exactly the same reason." Manley estimated that as a result of this migration, some "$300 million have left Jamaica illegally" (*Daily Gleaner,* 6 January 1977, 7). Yet Manley himself and others in his government had previously displayed a certain indifference toward this exodus, proclaiming that there were five flights a day to Miami available for anyone who wished to leave Jamaica. Manley's rhetoric of "democratic socialism" was antagonistic to the private sector, and on many occasions it induced violence against businesspeople, who were depicted as exploiting ordinary Jamaicans. As a result, many businesspeople abandoned their businesses and emigrated to the United States.

For other observers, however, the impact of the managerial and professional brain drain was perceived as unambiguously negative. Margaret Morris, for instance, writing in the *Daily Gleaner* in 1979, noted that brain drain had hit the local airline, Air Jamaica, very hard. "They have lost, in rapid succession, a competent Jamaican president and three of [their] most competent top executives. This year they lost 45 members of the staff, most from Customer Service, an area which was already weak. They seem to have no shortage of executives but very few middle managers. Whenever something goes wrong harassed passengers are unable to find any ranking person to appear or reassure them, and are left wondering if the supervisors have run away or simply don't exist" (Morris 1979, 30).

Another perception was that emigration had decimated the ranks of a deserving group of professionals:

> The Jamaica managerial cadre at present represents the first set of poor Jamaicans who have made it from humble village and primary school into the board room. In less than ten years, we have moved from a dominance of foreign bank managers, for instance, to a position now where only a handful of senior banking executives are foreigners. It is the managerial group, indeed, who have moved furthest and who have gained most from the political upheaval which began in 1938. It is this group which has displayed the most uncertainty and has had the highest rate of emigration over the past few years. (*Jamaican Weekly Gleaner,* 3 July 1978, 15)

Even in the high-wage bauxite industry, the impact of the brain drain was assessed by one official as a major problem: "We are losing guys. They are emigrating. We are not losing them to companies here in Jamaica. We are losing them to the States, Canada and the U.K. and the disturbing part is not only are we losing professionals, we are losing technicians, we are losing trade skills and we are losing hourly paid operators. We have never had that happen before. And it's not that they are going one or two. We have heard lately that there are five electricians leaving one plant. We can't afford that" (*Jamaican Weekly Gleaner,* 10 July 1980, 13).

The seriousness of the migration problem was underscored by the *Gleaner,* the country's leading daily newspaper, in three different editorials between July 1978 and September 1979. Of the 43,000 who emigrated in 1976 and 1977 alone, the *Gleaner* was moved to write: "No one who is seriously interested in Jamaica's advancement could be pleased with this loss of skills. It is a loss that will be felt most critically as the economy makes an all out effort at recovery. For the professional skills and the experience which are lost to Jamaica are the very qualities which will be needed to lead research, planning, project implementation and development" (*Jamaica Weekly Gleaner,* 10 July 1980, 13).

Four months later, the *Gleaner* agonized about the problem: "There can be little doubt of Jamaica's need for highly skilled professionals and other personnel in important areas of industry, commerce, and health services and other professions. Of course, the situation has been severely aggravated by the rapid and continuing exodus of these skills from Jamaica, particularly over the past four years. The outward movement of such important skills constitutes a major drain on the country's investment in human resources, in effect Jamaica's loss is another country's gain (*Jamaican Weekly Gleaner,* 27 November 1978, 13).

Less than a year later, the *Gleaner* was alarmed by the sharp rise in the share of professional and managerial talent among the emigrants: "Obviously a serious phenomenon, it is compounded by the fact that unlike the trend in migration in earlier years, those leaving this country are mainly of the age ranging from 30–49 years, the group which possesses the experience and the dynamism so critically needed at this time" (*Jamaican Weekly Gleaner,* 24 September 1979, 13).

The impact of emigration on the operation of the public sector, particularly on the delivery of health services and on education, was devastating. In 1978, a report by the Private Sector Organization of Jamaica (PSOJ) described "the serious deterioration which is taking place at the University of the West Indies, particularly in the Medical Faculty, which concrete evidence indicates, is headed for possible collapse. In recent months an exceptionally large percentage of the staff has resigned, more are on the verge of quitting and, what is most alarming, no replacements can be found, despite repeated advertisements and personal appeals to West Indians and foreign personnel outside the region" (*Jamaican Weekly Gleaner,* 4 September 1978, 5).

The PSOJ viewed these developments as leading to the complete breakdown of the university hospital's ability to deliver valuable health services to the public. Beyond the university, the emigration of doctors and medical technicians seriously reduced the country's ability to deliver health services. Between 1974 and 1976, the number of doctors in the country declined from 570 to 390, reducing the doctor/population ratio from 1:3,553 to 1:5,314. The number of dentists also fell, from 107 to 84, reducing the dentist/population ratio from 1:18,925 to 1:22,000. These ratios were far below the doctor/population ratio of 1:910 and the dentist/population ratio of 1:2,857 recommended by the Pan American Health Organization (PAHO) (*Economic and Social Survey Jamaica 1979*).

In a rather unusual move, the *Gleaner* in one of its Sunday editions prefaced its "Career Opportunities" section with the following editorial:

> Jamaica continues to face the strange situation where there are thousands of unemployed, but at the same time there are several vacancies for skilled and qualified personnel. The migration of skills over the past two years has aggravated the shortage of skilled and experienced personnel, whereas the slowing down of the economy has hindered the creation of jobs for the recently qualified, the semiskilled and the unskilled. On this and other pages are advertisements of vacancies for the qualified. These vacancies must be filled. We bring them to your attention in the hope that the qualified will wish to avail themselves of these opportunities. We thank the organizations concerned for their advertisements of these vacancies. (*Sunday Gleaner,* 8 April 1979, 10)

Most of the jobs were of the managerial and supervisory kind, requiring previous experience ranging from two to five years. Most of the ads specified a preference for Jamaican nationals ranging in age from 30 to 40 years. In none of the ads were salaries stated, but most of them emphasized attractive salaries and fringe benefits. Because the professional and managerial emigrants fell largely within the ages of 30–40 years, it is reasonable to conclude that those remaining in Jamaica were in a strong position to command higher salaries. In view of the scarcity of professional people, some employers relaxed the nationality require- ment. At one point, the government, in an effort to replenish the depleted stock of medical specialists with expatriate doctors, advertised in the *British Medical Journal* a wide range of positions in the fields of pathology, psychiatry, internal medicine, orthopedic surgery, obstetrics and gynecology, urology, oral surgery and public health (*Jamaican Weekly Gleaner,* 17 April 1979, 13).

Any assessment of the impact of emigration on the countries of origin must be viewed not only against the background of what was happening in these countries but also against the background of what was happening in the larger world. Socialist governments had come to power in Jamaica (1972) and Guyana (1970) and proceeded to nationalize "the commanding heights" of the economy. This led to a serious diminution of the private sector and a drying up of private investment both foreign and domestic. Potential investors viewed the invest- ment climate as high risk because they feared their assets might be expropriated under a socialist government. The concentration of economic activity in the pub- lic sector led to mismanagement and waste. The oil crisis of the 1970s increased the cost of domestic production, and the worldwide recessions triggered by the sharp increase in oil prices reduced the demand for Caribbean exports and raised the cost of living as the higher cost of production was transmitted to higher prices for consumer goods. The deterioration in the nonoil Caribbean economy was therefore the result of a combination of domestic and internation- al factors. Against the background of these developments emigration took place.

A plausible argument can also be made that migration, especially the migra- tion of skilled people, accelerated the economic decline of Jamaica by depriving the productive units of the economy of valuable skills. This led to the underuti- lization of plant capacity. And when plant capacity remained underutilized for a long time it was often never brought back up because of the deterioration of equipment. As a consequence, the productive base of the economy shrunk. This means that the tax base also shrunk and the government was unable to raise enough revenues to finance its larger role in the economy. If emigration acceler- ated the decline in the economy, then it also accelerated the decline in living standards. This is particularly the case in the delivery of health services. The migration of doctors and nurses left hospitals understaffed, seriously curtailing the availability and quality of care. The fact is that the large inflows of private foreign capital during the 1960s obscured the negative effects of emigration. When those capital inflows dried up in the 1970s, the negative effects of skilled emigration became pronounced.

three

Settlement

In 1990, the U.S. Census counted 682,418 West Indians in America. This figure included immigrants from Barbados, Guyana, Jamaica, Trinidad and Tobago, and the smaller British West Indian islands, as well as the American-born children of those immigrants. The profile that emerges from the census tabulation in table 3.1 is that of a population with a median age of 33, 37 percent of whom are naturalized citizens, a male/female ratio of 83.0, and a median household income of $31,578.

The largest number of West Indians in the United States live in New York City. Although an increasing share settled in the Miami metropolitan area during the 1980s, New York City remains the preferred destination. Constance Sutton calls New York City "the Caribbean crossroads of the world. It contains the largest concentration and the most diverse commingling of its people" (Sutton 1987, 19). The greatest residential concentration in New York City is in the predominantly black neighborhoods of Brooklyn, where a common ethnic background and an established network of support systems provide a measure of security.

Oscar Handlin records that West Indian migration to the United States mainland rose in the decade after 1900, reaching some 40,000 by 1910, one quarter of whom were in New York City. By 1940, according to Handlin, the West Indian population in New York had grown to 50,000, adding significantly to the total black population in the city (Handlin 1959, 48–49). The migration of southern blacks to New York accelerated in the post-war period to meet labor shortages there, but the post-war growth of West Indian migration to the United States was slowed considerably by the McCarran-Walter Act of 1952, as mentioned in chapter 2. The impact of the act on West Indian immigration to the United States during the 1950s is shown in table 3.2.

According to Charles Green and Basil Wilson, West Indians were an influential group in Harlem during the 1930s. Their political and economic prominence at a time when Harlem was suffering from the Great Depression made them visible targets of resentment by black Americans (Green and Wilson 1989, 120–21). Even as late as the 1970s, one survey showed that the Caribbean business presence in Harlem was still marked: 14 percent of the black business owners were Caribbean born, the largest group after the southern born (Caplovitz 1973, 34). Miriam Klevan attributes the antagonistic relationship between American blacks and West Indians in the 1930s to the fact that "West Indian immigrants

Table 3.1

Profile of West Indians in America, 1990

Country of Ancestry	Total	Naturalized Citizens	Male/Female Ratio	Median Age	Median Household Income
Barbados	33,178	44.9%	81.7	37.4	$33,480
Guyana	75,765	38.4	87.4	30.6	33,904
Jamaica	410,933	37.9	85.4	31.4	30,461
Trin. and Tob.	71,720	28.0	80.4	32.1	30,305
Other Brit. West Indies	35,822	34.2	80.1	33.4	29,738
	682,418	Av: 36.7	Av: 83.0	Av: 33.0	Av: $31,578

Source: U.S. Bureau of the Census, *1990 Census of Population and Housing, CP-3-2, Ancestry of the Population of the United States: 1990.*

Table 3.2

West Indian Immigration to the United States, 1925–1970

Year of Immigration	No. of Immigrants	Change
1925–34	5,345	
1935–44	4,528	(817)
1945–49	10,158	5,630
1950–54	13,149	2,991
1955–59	15,588	2,439
1960–64	39,848	24,260
1965–70	112,657	72,809

Source: U.S. Department of Commerce, Bureau of the Census, *1970 Census of the Population: National Origin and Language,* Final Report PC(2)-1A (Washington, D.C., U.S. Government Printing Office, 1973).

were generally status conscious and often looked down on American blacks for their lack of education." American blacks, on other hand, mocked the cultural snobbery of West Indians, calling them "monkey chasers," "Jewmaicans," "Garveyites," and "cockneys" (Klevan 1990, 44). Nathan Glazer and Daniel Patrick

Moynihan sum up the impact of the Depression on Harlem this way: "Dependent on casual labor and household service, without salaried jobs, without businesses, Harlem's residents suffered far more from the depression than any other part of the city" (Glazer and Moynihan 1963, 28).

West Indian migration to Brooklyn (as opposed to Harlem) began about 1940. After a period of slow growth during the 1950s, migration accelerated during the 1960s, when the achievement of political independence removed the former British colonies from the restricting colonial quotas. This growth in immigration caused West Indian settlements to spread from Crown Heights into East Flatbush and parts of Flatbush. (Bogen 1987, 72). The 1970 U.S. Census reported 171,525 immigrants from the West Indies in New York City. This represented 73 percent of all the West Indian immigrants in the United States, 48 percent of whom arrived between 1965 and 1970. The 1980 U.S. Census data show that in addition to Jamaicans, there was a sharp increase in the number of Haitians and Guyanese in central Brooklyn. Bogen points out that the deterioration in housing conditions and commercial rent that resulted from the increased population density was arrested by the West Indian population, which "has long been renowned for its thrift, industry, and skillful property management" (Bogen 1987, 73).

The West Indian Community

The majority of the West Indians in Brooklyn live in black enclaves and rarely interact socially with the white population. In her comparison of Jamaicans in New York and London, Nancy Foner observes that "New York Jamaicans, submerged in the wider black community, move in a more 'black' social world than their London counterparts. At the same time, however, Jamaicans in New York differentiate themselves from indigenous blacks. The net result is that their position as black Jamaicans is less painful and their contacts with whites more limited than in London. It is also easier for them to participate in many activities" (Foner 1987, 10).

While West Indian immigrants have maintained an ethnic identity separate from the rest of the black population, they nevertheless identify with the major civil rights issues that affect blacks in American society. Constance Sutton makes the observation that "Caribbean peoples in New York City are not readily induced to shed their cultural heritages or separate Caribbean-based identities as they seek to further their socio-economic status in New York" (Sutton 1987, 21). Yet because they come to the United States with the goal of improving their socioeconomic status, they must necessarily assimilate into the American workplace.

Beyond the workplace, they strive to maintain their West Indianness and therefore their separate cultural identity. The principal institution around which this is accomplished is the family. Around the immigrant family is a network of associations woven into the ethnic fabric of the community. Because the influence of American culture is overwhelming in their daily lives and because West Indians are often not identifiable amidst the larger black population (Bryce-Laporte 1972, 29–56), the West Indian community must regularly put its ethnic distinctiveness on display for the rest of the society to see. The most expressive display has been in the form of music and dance, which are colorfully brought together at annual festivals and carnivals.

The carnival was originally a pre-Lenten festival, but in its adaptation to the areas of settlement in the temperate zone, it has become a summer ritual. In Toronto, the Caribbean festival winds through the heart of the city like a stream of merriment. In Washington, D.C., it is often a part of the Smithsonian Institution's Folklife Festival on the Mall in July. In Brooklyn, where the largest number of West Indians in America live, the West Indian American Day Carnival is celebrated each year on Labor Day.

For Americans, Labor Day signals the end of summer. It is a day of picnics and speeches and parades honoring the American worker and the American labor movement. For the West Indian immigrant, it is a day off from the melting pot of the workplace. The West Indian American Day Carnival in Brooklyn does not celebrate the end of anything; it celebrates the presence of West Indians as a distinct ethnic group. It is their annual step out of the melting pot.

The essence of the West Indian American Day Carnival is music and dance. Immigration and Naturalization Service statistics show that from 1962 to 1972—a period that included the first surge of immigration after the 1965 Immigration and Nationality Act—135 musicians and music teachers were among the professional immigrants to the United States from the English-speaking Caribbean. In their cultural baggage and that of the tens of thousands who arrived later, they brought with them the musical sounds and dances of home. The West Indian American Day Carnival along Brooklyn's Eastern Parkway is the public unpacking of this cultural baggage. In this participatory ritual, many of the players are elaborately disguised in the costumes of mythical figures dancing to the tropical rhythms of the carnival steel band. The carnival is not meant to be watched; it is to be participated in. It is not an orderly parade that passes by in a timely fashion. It is a revelry that gathers people in as it floats along. Although the West Indian carnival is largely Trinidadian in origin, in America it has become truly West Indian as it embraces those from other islands. Thus in New York—the crossroads of the Caribbean—the carnival is a potent symbol of West Indian solidarity.

While West Indians strive to maintain their ethnic and cultural identity in America, their socioeconomic success depends on the larger black population. In her comparative study of Jamaicans in New York and London, Nancy Foner argues that the presence and residential concentration of so many American blacks in cities where West Indians live benefits West Indian business enterprises by providing them with a ready-made market (Foner 1987, 125). But the business success of West Indians involves more than that. Bryce-Laporte attributes their success to their "aspirations, sense of purpose, desire and detachment they bring with them, the relative absence of inhibiting socialization, the close family or indigenous support systems which they retain and their willingness to sacrifice to meet their ends" (Bryce-Laporte 1972, 2). And because they come from societies where institutional saving in the form of social security taxes is a relatively recent innovation, they have not lost the zest for private cooperative saving arrangements, as Aubrey Bonnett has documented among first-generation West Indians in Brooklyn (Bonnett 1981).

Shirley Chisholm, the first black woman to be elected to the U.S. Congress, writes in her autobiography, *Shirley Chisholm: Unbought and Unbossed,* that one basis for the success of people of West Indian ancestry in New York "may be that in the islands, slavery was a less destructive experience than it was in the States.

Families were not broken up as they were in the South. The abolition of slavery came earlier there, and with much less trouble. In the islands, there have never been the same kind of race barriers. There are class barriers, but they are not the same; race lines cut across them. As a result, I think blacks from the islands tend to have less fear of white people, and therefore less hatred of them. They can meet whites as equals; this is harder for American blacks, who tend to over-react by jumping from feeling that whites are superior to looking down on them as inferior. Both attitudes isolate them from the greater society in which eventu-ally we all have to live." (Chisholm 1970, 90)

Because of their economic success and strong orientation to community val-ues, the West Indians stand out in sharp contrast to the surrounding native black population. James Traub describes these differences in Brooklyn:

> At the northwestern edge of Brooklyn lies that part of Rutland Road adjacent to Brownsville. Here Rutland Road is roughly 75 percent West Indian; Brownsville is almost all native American black. In Browns-ville, homes and stores lie abandoned, drug addicts and winos are easy to spot, crime is part of daily life. The residents of Rutland Road speak of Brownsville as if it were some kind of plague. Rutland Road is no model community either: the stores have a distinctly drab and under-patronized look to them. Yet it is a community of homeowners, shop-keepers, blue-collar workers. Two hospitals in the area provide a base of employment. And on either side of the commercial street are rows and rows of well-kept two-family homes, with fenced-in gardens, looking out over immaculate streets. Everywhere signs advertise block associations, neighborhood patrols. When a house comes up for sale, people try to reserve it for a friend or relative . . . Elsewhere in Brooklyn, and elsewhere in America's big cities, the iron law of white flight and subsequent decay can be seen working its way out; but not in West Indian districts. (Traub 1982, 27)

Two objectives drive West Indians to work long and hard hours: owning a house and getting an education. As Traub observes: "They work fanatically hard, save money, and get an education, if not for themselves, then for their children" (Traub 1982, 28). Thus the willingness to sacrifice leisure for work and the present for the future has been a powerful force behind the advance-ment of West Indians as a group. The economic base provided by this sacrifice has allowed the second and third generations of West Indians to assimilate socially into the American mainstream to a greater degree than the first gener-ation. Dennis Forsythe suggests that the degree to which West Indians (or for that matter any other ethnic group) assimilate is influenced by the similarity of their cultural orientation to that of America's. Forsythe attributes the measure of West Indian success in America to the fact that "every phase and aspect of the West Indian experience have imbued them with the Protestant 'spirit'" (Forsythe 1976, 65). What makes the West Indian achievement seem remark-able is the generally low expectations of blacks held by the majority of Americans. Indeed, it is because of these low expectations that West Indians wish to be seen as a separate ethnic group.

Unsure of their ties with the host society, West Indians preserve their ties with their countries of origin. This is done through frequent contacts with relatives and friends back home as well as through their many associations in their immigrant community. It is said that the coming of direct-dial telephone service between the United States and the Caribbean in the 1970s has greatly facilitated these ties. Of the immigrants in the United States, West Indians are among the most frequent visitors to their home countries. The connection with home, which becomes more romantic as years pass, provides important psychological support for people not fully assimilated into their host society. In a survey of West Indians in Los Angeles, Joyce B. Justus made the following observation: "The West Indian looks to his homeland and to the local West Indian community in the United States for much of his acceptance or rejection, praise or blame, recognition for past achievements and support for his aspirations" (Justus 1976, 145).

There are two identifiable layers of West Indian associations—the country associations whose members are nationals from a particular country and the pan-Caribbean or pan–West Indian associations whose membership comes from the larger regional groupings. Although the primary concern of the country associations has been "making it in America," as Thomas observes, they have maintained strong ties with the home country, often raising funds for projects, sponsoring trips, and hosting visiting politicians (Thomas 1988, 53). Some are tied to political organizations back home such as the Jamaica Progessive League.

Founded by Wilfrid Domingo and Walter Adolphe Roberts and other Jamaican residents in New York in 1936, the league is affiliated with the People's National Party in Jamaica. Its Marxist and anti-colonial ideas were an important influence on early political developments in Jamaica. In Morley Ayearst's assessment, "The pre-party Jamaican nationalist movement had important roots in the United States and substantial monetary support has been given, year after year by former Jamaicans, now American residents, to [the] People's National Party" (Ayearst 1960, 135). League founder Wilfrid Domingo testified before the Moyne Commission, which was sent by Britain to investigate the social and economic conditions in Jamaica in 1938. The league was also active in securing legal defense for many who were charged in the rioting that year (Thomas 1988, 53). When Jamaica gained its political independence in 1962, the league lobbied the U.S. Congress to have Jamaica declared a nonquota country under the McCarran-Walter Act of 1952. The league today is a shadow of its former self. Its membership has dwindled considerably and so has its political influence.

In the aftermath of a natural disaster in the Caribbean, such as a hurricane, West Indian associations usually swing into action to provide material aid. They also are seen to perform as "overseas trade development corporations for the Caribbean islands," encouraging trade between the United States and the Caribbean and even trying to influence American businesses to relocate in the region (Thomas 1988, 53).

The pan–West Indian associations are the ones that generally interact with the host society. Among these are the Caribbean American Chamber of Commerce and Industry and the West Indian American Day Carnival Association, both in New York, and the Caribbean American Intercultural Organization in Washington, D.C. These pan-Caribbean groups regularly organize the cultural events that define West Indians in the United States as a distinct ethnic community. While the existence of country associations, with their strong ties to individual home countries, may place certain constraints on the development of pan–West Indian organizational structures, Linda Basch argues that the "the political linkages that they maintain with their home societies create an alternate area of political action and acknowledged prestige that can in turn serve as a mobilizing force for organizational activities in New York" (Basch 1987, 177).

Like many ethnic groups in America, West Indians have placed a high value on their cultural heritage. They have maintained their linkage to their home countries through their associations. This bond has sustained them in their efforts to build their lives from scratch in a new society. But as subsequent generations move into the American mainstream, they also move away from the residential concentration that gave life to the associations.

The associations are kept alive primarily by first-generation immigrants. It is they who never fully assimilate, and it is they who try hardest to preserve their ties with their home countries. In an important sense, these immigrants find themselves suspended between two worlds—the world of their host country, in which they are not fully assimilated, and the world of their home country, where they are regarded as expatriates. This suspended existence has caused many to swing back and forth between the two worlds like a pendulum. The swing over to the home country is usually motivated by the remembrance of things past, and the swing back by the obligations of the present and the promise of the future.

This state of suspension is also a state of political disenfranchisement for most immigrants. Once they emigrate, most are not permitted to vote back home, except in the case of Guyana, where Guyanese citizens can vote in Guyana's national elections. In America they cannot vote if they are not citizens, and to become a citizen usually takes five or more years. Thus one of the personal costs of immigration is the loss of political enfranchisement. In this sense, the West Indian may view migration as a return to the colonial past—a time without voting rights. Thus the paradox of contemporary migration to America is that the West Indian has moved from a nineteenth-century to a twentieth-century economy only to encounter a nineteenth-century political past. The fact that many West Indians have been willing to pay this price is testimony to the power of economic opportunities over political enfranchisement. But this state of disenfranchisement is a major force that pulls West Indians together as a community. Their participation in their various associations substitutes for the political power they lack. Although individual West Indians have achieved prominent political positions at the local and national levels in the past, the fact is that there is a wide gap between their economic prowess and their political influence today.

First generation West Indians, even when they achieve high economic and social status, tend to maintain a certain psychological distance between themselves and the rest of the American society. Justus explains this phenomenon as follows: "Given their immigrant status, distinct socialization experiences and oft times transient orientations, these West Indians may adopt instrumental attitudes and psychological distance towards the American society, its institutions and even its black community. This enables them to tolerate and withstand even anticipated forms of prejudice and discrimination in the pursuit of their objectives. But in doing so, generally, they do not accept the view of themselves as negative individually or as a group" (Justus 1976, 143).

Over the years, this psychological distance has made many West Indians reticent about becoming naturalized citizens. Those who arrived after 1960 have one of the lowest rates of naturalization of all the immigrant groups in the United States. This is so even for West Indians whose home countries allow for dual citizenship. This low rate of naturalization has limited the growth of their electoral influence; if they are not citizens, they cannot vote. Table 3.3 shows that the percent of naturalized West Indians declined sharply between 1925 and 1970.

These tendencies notwithstanding, a number of West Indians in New York achieved a considerable measure of political success. In the 1960s, Bertram L. Baker, who was born on the island of Nevis, became the first black state assemblyman from Brooklyn. And Shirley Chisholm, the first black woman elected to the U.S. Congress, became the most prominent politician of West Indian heritage in America. In her autobiography, she writes that "a surprising number of black politicians of our time are of West Indian descent. Thomas Jones, Ruth Goring, William Thompson and I were all of Barbadian descent. State senator Walter Stewart of Brooklyn is a Panamanian. So are many prominent blacks elsewhere and in the arts." She recalls that in Brooklyn, "I have heard people grumbling for years, 'They're taking over everything.' Other black people will say 'Why don't those monkeys get back on a banana boat?' There is a strong undercurrent of resentment, at least in New York, where most islanders migrated. It

Table 3.3

Percent of Naturalized West Indian Immigrants, 1925–1970 and 1990

Year of Immigration	No. of Immigrants	% Naturalized
1925–34	5,245	89.0
1935–44	4,528	89.2
1945–49	10,158	85.8
1950–54	13,149	76.2
1955–59	15,588	55.9
1960–64	39,848	31.0
1965–70	112,657	15.3
All immigrants in 1990	682,418	36.7

Sources: U.S. Department of Commerce, Bureau of the Census, *Census of the Population, 1970: National Origin and Language,* Report PC(2)-1A (Washington, D.C., U.S. Government Printing Office, 1973); *1990 Census of Population and Housing,* CP-3-2, *Ancestry of the Population in the United States: 1990.*

has never come out in the open against me, but sometimes I can sense it" (Chisholm 1970, 89).

Today West Indian–born Mervyn Dymally, former lieutenant governor of California, is a Democratic congressman. By far the most prominent person of West Indian heritage in America today is General Colin Powell, former chairman of the Joint Chiefs of Staff, whose parents are Jamaican. On the intellectual front, two Nobel laureates, both from St. Lucia, economist W. Arthur Lewis and poet Derek Walcott, received their prizes while living in America, although they completed their major works elsewhere.[1]

Prior to the 1960s, black American and West Indian political alliance was galvanized by the virulence of racial discrimination and the quest for civil rights. Ethnicity took a back seat to the pressing racial issues of the time. Thomas points out that in that spirit of cooperation, "Caribbean associations made every effort to know African Americans, their experiences and history" (Thomas 1988, 50). This was not the case historically: in the 1920s sharp ideological differences were played out between West Indian Marcus Garvey and the black intellectuals of Harlem.

In Harlem, Garvey saw the political future of blacks as a separate black nation in Africa and their economic future determined by black capitalism. The black intellectuals saw music and the arts as the vehicle for portraying the power of black culture and they saw Africa as a distant cultural heritage from which they could draw to enrich their own culture at home. The black intellectuals were well educated. They included W. E. B. DuBois, James Weldon Johnson, Wallace Thurman, Alain Locke, Zora Neal Hurston, Jessie Fausset, and Rudolph Fisher. Garvey's critics were not exclusively American blacks, however; they included the West Indian writer Claude McKay (Runcie 1986, 7–11).

Many of these intellectuals had done graduate work; W. E. B. DuBois and Alain Locke had doctoral degrees from Harvard University. Marcus Garvey was a Jamaican who had not finished his grade school. He was a stubby, dark-skinned black man of five feet, six inches, while his intellectual opponents were for the most part extremely light skinned; some could have passed for white. Garvey questioned their commitment to racial pride, especially in view of the fact that they made their living writing about the desperate conditions of blacks and selling their works to white publishers. The intellectuals pilloried Garvey and in some sense were jealous of his tremendous power over the black masses of Harlem. They called him names such as "buffoon" and "monumental monkey." Garvey often responded in kind, on one occasion calling DuBois "an unfortunate mulatto" (Runcie 1986, 7–11).

Garvey founded the weekly newspaper *Negro World* and the United Negro Improvement Association (UNIA), and he fired the imagination of many with his plan to establish the Black Star Line Steamship Company, which was to transport blacks to the new nation in Africa over which he was to preside. The black intellectuals submitted no work for publication in *Negro World*, preferring instead to publish in such black organs as *Crisis, Opportunity,* and *Messenger.* Garvey staged grand parades, dressed in imperial costumes, and conferred knighthood on members of his UNIA for a fee. Some say his extravagant behavior was his way of compensating for his limited education, but it drew ridicule from those who opposed him.

As a visionary, Garvey raised the hopes of the black masses. He showed oppressed blacks that through self-reliance they could rise above the ordinary. Like all visionaries, Garvey did not encumber his grand design with such troubling questions as why American blacks would want to resettle in a place they had never been or why Africans would be willing to accept them. Garvey's thinking was that blacks could not prosper as a minority in a predominantly white country, and it was influenced by the resettlement of American freed slaves in Liberia as colonists in 1822. But since that time there has been seething resentment of their dominance by native Africans, who in 1980 overthrew the ruling descendants of those settlers. Garvey's Black Star Line went bankrupt, and in 1925 he was convicted and imprisoned for fraud. After serving two years in prison in Atlanta he was deported to Jamaica. Gordon K. Lewis sums up Garvey and his movement as follows: "He openly challenged the reigning false standards of racial values. Equally, he was the pioneer of organized political party life, for he demonstrated, in Kingston as in Harlem, that the Negro could be organized and that he was eager to repose confidence in and support [for] sincere Negro leadership" (Lewis 1968, 177).

Throughout the twentieth century, the West Indian immigrant voice in America has consistently spoken for racial pride. In the 1920s, it was the centerpiece of the Marcus Garvey movement; in the 1960s, "black is beautiful" became the rallying cry of another West Indian, Stokely Carmichael.

As civil rights receded as the galvanizing political force for black Americans and West Indians in the 1960s and as the size and concentration of the West Indian population in New York City grew, West Indians began to perceive their political interest in ethnic terms. As a result, they have now acquired the behavior of a special interest group whose principal agenda is not so much to achieve political power but to influence the power structure. But in this endeavor, their alliance with black Americans is essential. As Basch puts it, "Black Americans remain an important reference group and mediating force for West Indians when it comes to their dealings with the wider society, particularly in applying pressure on host institutions for goods, positions, and other rewards" (Basch 1987, 178).

Green and Wilson express the view that "the fear on the part of black elected officials [in New York City] is that the rise of Caribbean nationalism could drive a wedge in the black movement and weaken the struggle for black empowerment" (Green and Wilson 1989, 123). While this fear may be real in New York City, it certainly is not the case nationally, where West Indians represent a small share of the total black population. Moreover, the struggle for black empowerment at the political level has made great strides over the past quarter century, as evidenced by the number of black Americans who have been elected mayors in many large cities, some of them with minority black populations.

A Profile of Two Communities

Although the vast majority of West Indian immigrants have settled in the New York City and Miami metropolitan areas, a substantial number are to be found in other metropolitan areas, such as Chicago, Philadelphia, Detroit, Baltimore, Washington, D.C., and Hartford, Connecticut. The West Indian communities in the latter two areas are of particular interest, Washington for its high share of professionals and Hartford for its origin and development. The purpose here is to provide a sketch of the principal characteristics of these two communities to underscore the diversity among West Indian immigrant groups in America.

Of the West Indian communities in the United States, the one in the Washington area has the largest share of professionals. The resident West Indian population, estimated at about 10,000, is employed in a wide range of occupations in federal, state, and local governments and in private institutions. This population is augmented by a nonimmigrant corps of West Indians who are international civil servants at the World Bank, the International Monetary Fund, the Organization of American States, and the InterAmerican Development Bank, as well as by a floating population of diplomatic personnel and students. The private institution with the single largest concentration of West Indian professionals is Howard University, where they are professors, administrators, and support staff. Over the years, the university has trained may Caribbean dentists, physicians, and pharmacists and has developed as an important intellectual link between black America and the Caribbean and between black Americans and the West Indian-Amercan community. The university also provides a symbolic political and cultural link when it plays host, as it often does, to visiting Caribbean political leaders and Caribbean cultural events.

Like other immigrants, the Caribbean intellectuals at Howard maintain strong ties with their countries of origin through their research on a variety of problems in the region. This represents, on the one hand, a kind of intellectual remittance to the Caribbean, and on the other, a contribution to the host society's knowledge of the region. Despite the philosophical diversity of their research, especially in the social sciences, a common view that seems to emerge among these scholars is that cooperation between the United States and the Caribbean is essential and that the Caribbean perspective on its future development must inform any United States decision to assist the region.

Caribbean immigrant intellectuals, like those from other parts of the world, occupy a special perch in the United States. Not only do they view their countries of origin from a different vantage point but they must also reconcile their research interest with their professional advancement in the host country. They are confronted as immigrants with what Henry Grunwald calls a "double life and double vision," which over time tend to "converge into a single state of mind" (Grunwald 1985, 101).

The West Indians living in Washington can be called a community only in the loosest sense. Scattered residentially throughout the area, the West Indian population is linked informally through various social and cultural organizations. Community growth has been fed by students who have settled in the area after their university training and by professional West Indians from other parts of the United States. Although the share of immigrants who come directly from the Caribbean is relatively small, the area has received roughly the same number of West Indian immigrants (mostly Jamaicans) as such traditional destinations as Hartford throughout the latter half of the 1980s.

The West Indian community in Hartford is more tightly knit. This is largely due to its origins. It began in the 1940s with a handful of farm workers who picked tobacco and apples in the Connecticut Valley. By the end of the 1980s, the community had developed into a thriving population of some 25,000. Seventy percent of them are from Jamaica. Community leaders emphasize that an important element in their success is the respect the early members won from the larger community through hard work, earnestness, and an easy adaptation to middle class living. Although the founding community members were recruited as farm workers, many of them had high-school educations and had come from middle-class families in Jamaica who owned their own homes. They had taken advantage of the farm worker program during the war to widen their horizons and ultimately to exploit opportunities outside of farming. Thus while they had come as temporary migrants, they were able to set down roots. Many of them skipped their farm work contract and remained in the country illegally for years. Some were able to regularize their status by virtue of spouses or offspring born in the United States. Others had accumulated enough assets to convince immigration authorities that they were not a drain on the public purse.

As an ethnic immigrant community, the West Indians in Hartford are well organized. Two institutions reflect this organization: the West Indian Social Club and the Caribbean-American Society. Both own their own buildings. The facilities of the West Indian Social Club are said to be the largest of any Caribbean group in the United States, with the capacity to accommodate 800 people for a variety of functions. The building is estimated to be worth upward of $1 million and was purchased as a joint investment venture by members of the community.

These organizations and their buildings reflect not only the cultural presence of the community in Hartford but also its economic success. The community is for the most part solidly middle class, and many live outside of Hartford's city limits. In Hartford itself West Indians have moved into areas once occupied by white ethnic groups. The economic presence of the West Indian community may be directly observed along Albany Avenue in Hartford, where a plethora of small businesses evokes Spanish Town Road in Jamaica, a main commercial thoroughfare leading into the capital, Kingston. In private-sector employment, many West Indians work as professionals in finance, insurance, and real estate.

The church has played an important role in the life of the West Indian community. In the early days, many who were Catholics met and organized social events at St. Benedict's Catholic Church. It was from these meetings that the West Indian Social Club emerged. Among the founding members of the Hartford community was Alfred Lambert, vicar of St. Monica's Church. Today, West Indians continue to play an important role in the church. For example, the suffragan bishop of the Episcopal Church of Hartford, Clarence Poolridge, is a Guyanese. In addition to being a hard-working people, West Indians in Hartford also describe themselves as "church-going."

The hard work and earnestness that have shaped their economic success have also shaped the political orientation of their leaders. The only West Indian to be elected to the Hartford City Council, Colin Bennett, ran as a Republican and was elected four times. And the president of the Hartford chapter of the Jamaica Progressive League, which is affiliated with the socialist People's National Party in Jamaica, is also a Republican. There appears to be a right of center drift in the politics of this middle class community.

Currently, there is no West Indian on the Hartford City Council, and this has been a source of concern. In August 1989, the *Hartford Courant* reported that a group of 100 people gathered at the West Indian Social Club as part of the West Indian Independence celebrations to "learn from local politicians how the West Indian community could gain political power" (Richardson 1989, D3). Many in the community seem to feel that despite their economic achievements, they have been left out of the political process and that as hard-working, tax-paying citizens they need to be involved. The situation was summed up succinctly by one member of the audience: "The problem is we're busy trying to pay the mortgage, pay the tuition for Catholic schools—trying to make ends meet—we need to know how to become busy getting involved in the political process. We've got to be fired up with energy, and then we'll get someone on the council" (Richardson 1989, D3). The concern expressed by West Indians in Hartford may be viewed as the natural political awakening of a community after it has arrived at a certain economic threshold.

The experience of ethnic groups in Lowell, Massachusetts, may have some lessons for West Indians in Hartford. Shirley Kolack writes that "by the turn of the century, the Irish in Lowell, Lawrence, and other Merrimack Valley Communities began to gain status. The increase in numbers, and the acceptance of the Protestant Ethic expressed in their willingness to do the hardest and dirtiest work, spurred their movement up the ladder." But upward mobility became more difficult in Lowell as each ethnic group making progress proceeded to discriminate against those that followed. As the Irish moved up, Kolack continues, "they took on the role of the oppressor as a new wave of immigration made up of French Canadians spread over the Merrimack Valley" (Kolack 1980, 341). Contemporary immigrant groups must therefore fight harder to advance and to share power with those who currently hold it. While West Indians' ethnicity might once have been a positive force in the economic development of their community, with only 17 percent of the Hartford population, they will have to transcend ethnic separatism and build cross-ethnic coalitions to foster political development.

four

Occupation, Employment, and the Economic Status of the Immigrants

Occupational Background and Employment

The relationship between the structure of employment in the destination economy and the occupational structure of incoming immigrants is not a simple one because the occupation declared by the immigrant on arrival may not be the one in which he or she finds a job. It is generally argued that the immigrant undergoes an occupational downgrading on coming to the United States because job qualification requirements are higher here. Someone who is an elementary school teacher in the Caribbean without a bachelor's degree may declare his or her occupation on arrival as a school teacher but would not be able to find a job as a school teacher. Even in the medical professions, doctors and nurses are required to pass state examinations before they are allowed to practice.

Many professionals have the advantage of having been trained in America, so that by the time they are officially classified as immigrants (instead of as foreign students), they are already certified to practice. In the case of medical professionals, even if they were trained in the Caribbean, they are able to take their certifying examinations before they migrate. This is particularly true for immigrant nurses, who are able to move immediately into the practice of their profession. It is reasonable to argue that among all the occupational groups, those in the medical professions are least likely to suffer from occupational downgrading.

The Decline of Manufacturing and the Rise of the Service Sector

The distribution of occupations in the destination economy indicates the structure of the demand for workers to which the supply of immigrant workers must eventually conform. This means a concentration of immigrant workers in the lower rung of the service occupations. The service sector produces what economists call "nontradable" goods, meaning goods not traded internationally, as opposed to "tradable" goods, which are. Health and construction services, for example, must be consumed where they are produced, whereas manufactured goods may be produced in one country and consumed in another. Unlike manufacturing industries, service industries typically must produce their services on location and therefore cannot move elsewhere in search of low-cost labor; the low-cost labor must come to them.[1] Thus we have the phenomenon of many producers of tradable goods moving in search of low-cost labor, often in foreign countries, and low-cost foreign labor migrating in search of jobs largely in service industries.

Since the 1970s, the sharp devaluation of Caribbean currencies vis-à-vis the U.S. dollar has made the low cost of Caribbean labor attractive to many offshore American manufacturing operations, particularly in the textile and apparel industry. It has also sharply increased the cost of living in the Caribbean and widened the disparity between the wage rates in offshore manufacturing and those in the service sector of such places as New York City. As a result, the creation of jobs in offshore manufacturing operations in the Caribbean is not likely to reduce the flow of immigrants in search of jobs in the growing urban American service sector.

Women in the Service Sector

The service sector covers a wide diversity of employment, ranging from high-technology to low-skilled operations. A large share of the demand for workers in low-skilled jobs arises from the rapid growth of job opportunities for native-born American workers at the high-wage end of the service sector. As native-born workers move out of lower-paying jobs and into the more attractive, higher-paying jobs, immigrant workers move in to fill the employment vacuum. In some instances, new low-wage jobs are created by two-earner families. "The return of many middle class women to the workforce in the 1970's," writes Philip Kasinitz, "created a huge need for domestic workers," to which he attributes the growth of private household employment among West Indian women (Kasinitz 1988, 194).

It may also be argued that the opening of job opportunities in nontraditional occupations for native-born women has created a movement away from such traditional occupations as nursing. This in turn has created a shortage of nurses that is being filled by immigrants. Here, where communication is critical, professional nurses from the English-speaking Caribbean enjoy an advantage. But even in lower-paying jobs, the command of English has its benefits. Kasinitz observes that the ability of West Indians in New York City to fit into the low-wage sector is enhanced by a "mastery of the English language that, in the eyes of many New Yorkers, is superior not only to that of other immigrants, but also to many native graduates of the New York public school system" (Kasinitz 1988, 192).

Migration from the Caribbean has traditionally been male dominated. The migrations to Panama to build the canal, to Costa Rica to build the railroad, and to Cuba to cut sugar cane all required the physical strength of males. Working conditions were invariably harsh and disease-ridden. Women began to migrate only when foreign households began to demand the services of domestics. The migration of women to Cuba as servants in the early part of the twentieth century was the first significant wave of female emigration for work. Likewise, in recent decades, the migration of women to Canada and the United States has been partly a response to the demand for domestic servants. Thus a large share of Caribbean women entered the labor force in these countries at the very lowest level.

Table 4.1

Share of Nurses in Professional and Technical Immigrants from the Caribbean, 1990–1992

Country	Prof. and Tech.	Nurses	Nurses as Percent of Prof. and Tech.
Jamaica	2,702	742	27.5
Trin. and Tob.	1,351	425	31.5
Barbados	218	50	23.0
Guyana	1,245	220	17.7
	5,516	1,437	26.0

Source: Statistics Division, U.S. Immigration and Naturalization Service.

The growth of the service sector in America in general and in New York in particular, however, has increased the demand for immigrant women in a wide range of occupations. As a result, the number of Caribbean women who have migrated as "principal aliens" over the past 10 years has increased. These women are not included in the immigration category of "housewives and dependents." Monica Gordon argues that "the present system of female migrant labor is more attractive to the capitalist sectors with low wage rates. Such women enter traditionally female sectors with low wage rates based on the concept of women's secondary function as earners" (Gordon 1990, 118).

The health services sector is a major employer of Caribbean women immigrants, with nurses representing the largest professional group. Table 4.1 shows that over the period 1990–92, 26 percent of the professional and technical immigrants from the four major English-speaking Caribbean countries were nurses. By far the largest concentration of immigrant women, however, was in clerical and private household services.

The Economic Progress of West Indian Immigrants

It has been argued that because the migration process generally tends to select the most resourceful, the population of immigrants will invariably contain a higher share of skilled people than the host population at large. And since skilled people earn more than unskilled people, the group with the largest share of skilled workers will generally be better off. While these arguments have some validity, they tend to neglect the tremendous obstacles faced by immigrants as they readjust their lives to earn a livelihood in a new society in which they inherit no assets but must create them to survive. What is more, not all West Indians who have been declared skilled in fact arrive with saleable skills. Furthermore, as table 4.2 shows, the degree of selectivity has declined somewhat over the years. Immigrant professionals admitted under the third preference[2] declined from 2.7 percent in 1970 to 1.5 percent in 1980, while immigrants

Table 4.2

Share of Immigrants Admitted into the United States under Occupational Preferences and Preferences for Relatives, 1970–1980

Year	Occupational Preferences		Relative Preferences
	All Occupations	Professionals (3d Pref.)	
1970	9.1 %	2.7%	24.7%
1974	7.2	2.0	24.0
1975	7.6	2.1	24.8
1976	6.6	2.1	25.6
1977	5.1	1.4	28.3
1978	5.1	0.8	31.6
1979	8.2	1.1	46.4
1980	8.3	1.5	40.8

Source: U. S. Bureau of the Census, *Statistical Abstract of the United States: 1982–83 and 1986* (Washington, D.C.: U.S. Government Printing Office, 1982 and 1985).

Table 4.3

Share of Professional and Technical Workers in Total Occupations of Immigrants from Jamaica at Time of Arrival and in 1980

Time of Arrival	Share at Time of Arrival	Share in 1980
1960–64	23.2[a]	15.8
1965–69	17.8	11.7
1970–74	13.1	8.5
1975–79	14.4	6.7

Sources: U.S. Bureau of the Census, Public Use Data, 1980, Statistical Division, Immigration and Naturalization Service, Washington, D.C.; U.S. Bureau of the Census, *Foreign-born Population in the United States: 1980 Census of the Population* (Washington, D.C.: Microfiche Technical Documentation, 1985).
[a]Average for the years 1962–64.

Table 4.4

Median Income of U.S. and Caribbean Households, 1980 and 1990

Country	1980	1990
Jamaica	$15,290	$30,461
Haiti	13,377	25,547
Barbados	12,279	33,480
Guyana	15,913	33,904
Trin. and Tob.	14,733	30,305
United States	17,710	30,056

Source: U.S. Bureau of the Census, *Foreign-born Population in the United States: 1980 Census of the Population* (Washington, D.C.: Microfiche Technical Documentation, 1985).
Note: The data for 1980 are for households with a Caribbean-born head and the data for 1990 are for households of Caribbean ancestry. The latter includes the children of immigrants who were born in the United States.

admitted under the preference for relatives increased from 24.7 percent to more than 40 percent. Table 4.3 shows that by 1980 each group of arrivals from Jamaica had experienced a decline in its share of professional and technical workers in total occupations, with the decline being greatest among the more recent arrivals.

Table 4.4 compares the median household income of the four major English-speaking Caribbean countries with that of the United States for 1980 and 1990. While the median household income of the United States was higher than that of each nationality group from the Caribbean in 1980, by 1990 all the Caribbean groups exceeded the median income for the United States.

Because the largest concentration of West Indians is in New York City and because wage rates are higher there than in other parts of the country, their incomes may be said to be distorted by location. Thus any comparison of their economic status with other groups not similarly located may overstate their economic status. To eliminate the influence of location, we compare the income of West Indians in New York State with that of the white population of the state. In this comparison, we also disaggregate the income of each nationality group by time of arrival. Table 4.5 shows that the median income of immigrants from the English-speaking Caribbean who arrived in 1960–64 and 1965–69 were generally at or near parity with that of whites in New York State. This means that it took 15–20 years for these immigrants to reach income parity with whites in the state.

While current income is an important measure of economic well-being, it is not by itself a complete measure. How people spend their incomes is critical for their future development and for that of their offspring. A high rate of savings usually enhances one's ability to eventually acquire large assets, such as a house. West Indians are property-owning people, and owning a house is a high priority for most of them. If they do not buy a house in America, they will save to buy

Table 4.5

Median Income of Households with Caribbean-born Head as a Percent of Median Household Income of Whites in New York State in 1980, by Year of Immigration

Countries	All Periods	Time of Arrival				
		1959 or Earlier	1960–64	1965–69	1970–74	1975–80
Caribbean	81.2	83.3	102.9	82.5	74.5	55.2
Jamaica	84.7	81.1	96.0	92.5	85.7	72.0
Haiti	74.1	84.4	100.6	86.9	71.7	50.2
Dom. Rep.	56.1	72.7	63.2	57.0	53.1	49.0
Barbados	79.1	65.8	85.3	104.5	81.2	62.8
Guyana	88.1	88.4	119.8	103.4	92.1	66.2
Trin. and Tob.	81.6	83.6	106.2	92.5	76.7	66.6

Sources: U.S. Bureau of the Census, *Foreign-born Population in the United States: 1980 Census of the Population* (Washington, D.C.: Microfiche Technical Documentation, 1985); U.S. Bureau of the Census, *1980 Census of the Population: General Social and Economic Characteristics: New York* (Washington, D.C.: U.S. Government Printing Office, 1983).

one in their country of origin. West Indians have developed a reputation for being thrifty. Although no data on their savings rate are available, their high rate of home ownership in Brooklyn and Hartford tends to confirm this.

A Comparison of American- and Foreign-Born West Indians with the General U.S. Population

Thomas Sowell cites the economic success of West Indians in America to underscore his argument that blacks can be successful in spite of racism (Sowell 1975). Some view any income comparison between West Indians and black Americans as flawed on the grounds that West Indians are concentrated in the Northeast and Miami, where wages are high, and that the selectivity of the migration process gives them an edge (Green and Wilson 1989, 123–24). Measures of income are nevertheless useful indicators of economic progress, and the identification of disparity in income between groups is usually the starting point of an investigation into its causes. (The following analysis draws heavily on relevant U.S. Census data for 1970, 1980, and 1990.)

In the New York City metropolitan area in 1970 both the American-born of West Indian parents and the foreign-born West Indians had higher median family incomes than the black population in general. The income gap between American-born West Indians and blacks was significantly greater than that between foreign-born West Indians and blacks. The median family income of the American-born West Indians was 94 percent that of whites, and the poverty rate for West Indian families was roughly half that of blacks and only a few percentage points above that of whites. It is clear from the data, then, that in 1970 the economic status of American-born West Indians in the New York metropolitan area was approaching parity with whites.

For the nation as a whole in 1970, the median family income of American-born West Indians ($10,624) had surpassed that of whites ($9,763). Furthermore, the poverty rate was lower: 10 percent compared with 11.6 percent for whites. The median family income of foreign-born West Indians was 98.5 percent that of whites nationwide. Thus, the West Indian population—both American-born and foreign-born—achieved in 1970 what the black population as a whole today has not.

A major reason for the success of the American-born West Indian population is the high share of professional and technical workers among its ranks—18.8 percent compared with 14.6 percent for whites and 8.1 percent for blacks in 1980. This is reflected in the median years of schooling completed, where the figure for the American-born West Indian exceeds that for whites.

American-born West Indians are second-generation immigrants who have acquired all of their education in the United States. The groups of foreign-born West Indians with annual incomes closest to them in 1980 were those who arrived in the United States between 1935 and 1944 ($10,189) and between 1960 and 1964 ($10,113). The median ages of these groups were 51.4 and 32.2 years, respectively, with the 1960–64 group reflecting a larger share of skilled immigrants. The median age of the American-born West Indian in 1980 was 18.5, the foreign born 34.4, the black American 22.1, and the white American 24.8. Thus the American-born West Indians were younger than white Americans and had higher median family incomes. For the age group 25 to 44, the median family income for American-born West Indians was $10,629, for foreign-born West Indians $8,423, and for black Americans $6,692. Thus the income gap between American-born and foreign-born West Indians was greater than the income gap between foreign-born West Indians and black Americans.

When all is said and done, the economic success of American-born West Indians must be attributed to their ethnic roots, to the investment in their education by their parents, and to the financial and real assets they may have inherited from their parents. Of the American-born West Indians, 12.8 percent had four or more years of college education, compared with 11.7 percent for whites and 4.2 percent for blacks. With this relatively high investment in education, American-born West Indians were poised to take advantage of the opportunities opened up by the civil rights movement of the 1960s, in which many of them and their parents had been active participants. The full employment of the 1960s also helped, allowing many American-born West Indians to achieve prominent positions. But in addition to the environmental conditions of civil rights and economic prosperity, the element of immigrant vitality and resourcefulness played a critical role in their advancement.

A Comparison of West Indians with Other Immigrant Groups

A complete examination of the progress of Caribbean immigrants in America should include a comparison with other successful immigrant groups. Such a comparison puts into better perspective the economic status of the Caribbean immigrant. Table 4.6 shows that the median income of Caribbean households in 1980 was below that of the major Asian immigrant groups and above that of the largest Latin American immigrant group—Mexicans. The disparity between Asian and Caribbean groups tended to widen the longer the immigrants were in America. To examine this phenomenon, we compare one Asian group—the Filipinos—with one Caribbean group—the Jamaicans.

The Philippines and Jamaica are good choices for comparison because each country represents the largest source of immigrants from its respective region and because the immigrants from each country share two important characteristics: they are able to speak English and they have among them a large share of health professionals. Over the four-year period between 1966 and 1969, for example, 2,240 nurses and 2,300 physicians and surgeons immigrated from the Philippines. Together, they represented a third of the inflow of Filipino professional and technical workers. Over the same period, 1,997 nurses and 64 physicians and surgeons immigrated from Jamaica, representing well over a third of the inflow of Jamaican professional and technical workers. Together, Jamaica

Table 4.6

Median Income of Households with Foreign-born Head in 1980 by Year of Arrival

Country	Total	1975-80	1970-74	1975-69	1960-64
Taiwan	$18,221	$10,221	$21,759	$29,494	$31,436
Philippines	26,666	20,579	28,559	32,596	32,116
Korea	18,258	14,420	21,326	24,093	20,291
Mexico	12,747	10,626	13,110	13,901	14,453
India	25,644	18,095	27,165	32,231	34,056
Cuba	16,326	6,595	13,932	15,143	19,877
Jamaica	15,290	13,003	15,484	16,717	17,333
Guyana	15,913	11,962	16,643	18,676	21,649
Trin. and Tob.	14,733	12,037	13,847	16,711	19,174
Barbados	14,290	11,341	14,673	18,875	15,417

Source: U.S. Bureau of the Census, *Foreign-born Population in the United States: 1980 Census of the Population* (Washington, D.C.: Microfiche Technical Documentation, 1985).

and the Philippines supplied the United States with 20 percent of its immigrant nurses over the four-year period. The Philippines alone provided 20 percent of the immigrant physicians and surgeons.

Of special interest are the occupational and economic status of those immigrants who arrived during the 1965–69 period, when there was a surge of immigration after the Immigration and Nationality Act of 1965. Our objective is to compare the progress of Filipinos and Jamaicans, using 1980 U.S. Census data, to put the progress of Jamaicans in particular and West Indians in general in better perspective.

As table 4.7 shows, time in the United States reduced the shares of professional and technical (PT) workers in both the Filipino and Jamaican groups. But even with this reduction, the PT shares for the Philippines are more than twice those for Jamaica. These differences are mirrored by the differences in median household income, with the disparity becoming larger the earlier the arrival. The widening of the income difference over time suggests that Filipino immigrants progressed more rapidly than Jamaican immigrants.

The Filipinos who arrived in the 1975–80 period had a median household income 58 percent higher than that of the Jamaicans, while those who arrived in the 1965–69 period had a median income almost twice as large. Yet the extent of the decline in the share of professional and technical workers among the Filipinos between their arrival and 1980 was sharper than that for the Jamaicans. Although the shares of PT workers are shown to decline between time of

Table 4.7

Median Household Income in 1980 and the Share of Professional and Technical (PT) Workers at Time of Arrival and in 1980, Philippines and Jamaica

| Time of Arrival | Median Household Income | | Share of PT Workers in Total Occupations | | | |
| | | | Philip. | | Jamaica | |
	Philip.	Jamaica	On Arrival	1980	On Arrival	1980
1960–64	$32,116	$17,333	47.9	26.5	23.2	15.8
1965–69	32,596	16,717	53.5	27.3	17.8	11.7
1970–74	28,559	15,484	65.3	22.0	13.1	8.5
1975–80	20,579	13,003	42.1	14.4	14.4	6.7
All groups	26,666	15,290				

Sources: U.S. Bureau of the Census, *Foreign-born Population in the United States: 1980 Census of the Population* (Washington, D.C.: Microfiche Technical Documentation, 1985); Statistical Division, Immigration and Naturalization Service, Washington, D.C.

arrival and 1980, the composition of the PT group may also have changed by 1980 in favor of more lucrative professions as a result of greater investment in education and training. It is also conceivable that the earliest arrivals were better educated, but in the absence of any evidence of a decline in the quality of education of the immigrants on arrival, we will stick to the original assumption of sharp occupational downgrading on arrival and rebuilding thereafter.

This is consistent with Barry R. Chiswick's observation that "the occupational mobility of male immigrants exhibits a U-shaped pattern; that is, occupational status declines when the 'last' occupation in the country of origin is compared with the 'early' U.S. occupation, after which upward occupational mobility is greater for the foreign born than for the native born" (Chiswick 1980, 24). Chiswick also points out that the intensity of the U-shaped pattern—that is, the steepness of the decline and rise-is greater for those immigrants with the least transferable skills, such as refugees, than for English-speaking economic immigrants with transferable skills.

While investment in education leads to higher incomes, the reverse is also true: higher incomes facilitate greater investment in education. Income, however, is not the only determinant of educational attainment. Such factors as family organization and the value placed on education as an instrument for social and economic advancement are also important. So even if household incomes were equal, the educational outcome may be unequal. But where there is significant disparity in household income, those households with higher incomes are generally in a better position to finance their children's education. As a result, the educational attainment of those children will generally be higher than those from lower income households.

Since there is a high correlation between education and income, investment in college education helps to explain the difference in median household income between the two groups. A measure of the extent to which those who arrived in 1965–69 invested in the college education of their children (15–19 year-olds then) after their arrival may be indicated by the share of the 26–34 year-olds who completed four or more years of college in 1980. In 1980, there were 18,846 Filipinos and 9,109 Jamaicans in this age group; 34 percent of the Filipinos and 17 percent of the Jamaicans had completed four or more years of college. It is clear, therefore, that the rate of investment in college education by Filipinos was twice that of Jamaicans. Given this higher rate of investment in college education, it is not surprising that the gap between the household incomes of the two immigrant groups widened with length of time in the United States.

But even on arrival, Filipino immigrants were earning significantly more than Jamaicans. This is largely due to the fact that they arrived with more education and training, which they received in an American-style public education system established when the United States ruled the Philippines as a colony for 50 years up to the end of World War II. According to Antonio Pido, "By 1956, the Philippines had the largest number of students at 1,560 per one hundred thousand of its population in the world. The country was, therefore, producing college graduates faster than the economy could absorb, most of whom were having different and higher outlooks and life styles than their parents" (Pido 1980, 348). Pido attributes the high share of professional and educated people among the Filipino immigrants to the selectivity of the immigration process: "In general, the qualificational selectivity of potential immigrants from the Eastern

Hemisphere tended to make the immigrants from this area professionals and from more affluent backgrounds" (Pido 1980, 349). Even when Filipinos do not pursue their profession in the United States and opt for lower-status jobs, Pido points out, their income and standard of living in the United States are relatively higher (Pido 1980, 351). The 1980 U.S. Census data show their median household income to be higher than that of Americans.

The above comparative analysis underscores the importance of education for income. But beyond that, it shows that the more educated an immigrant group is on arrival, the less competition it will face from other minority groups for jobs and the quicker it will move up the income scale. The analysis also suggests that the progress of Jamaicans in particular and West Indians in general might have been even greater had the share of college-educated people in their populations been greater and the increase in earnings resulting from additional investment in education larger. Using data from the 1970 U.S. Census of Population, Chiswick calculates that an additional year of schooling increased the earnings of Filipino adult male immigrants by an average of 6.4 percent, compared with 5.7 percent for white adult male immigrants and 3.3 percent for urban black adult male immigrants (Chiswick 1980, 24).

Kings County, New York

All migration from abroad is to local economies in the United States. While the flow of West Indians to Miami has increased somewhat over the last decade, most still head for New York City, where the economic opportunities are perceived to be better and where there is already a large West Indian population. Because the heaviest concentration of West Indian immigrants in America is in the New York City borough of Brooklyn in Kings County, it is important to document the demographic and economic environment of this destination.

In 1986, the population of Kings County was 2.3 million, 61 percent white and 34 percent black. Of the black population, 26 percent were foreign-born and 58 percent were women. The county has the lowest ratio of males to females in the State of New York. In 1984, there were 84.4 males to every 100 females. Among the Jamaican immigrants in Brooklyn this ratio was even lower. Table 4.8 shows that it ranged from a low of 75.3 for the age group 40–44 to a high of 87.1 for the age group 25–29 and averaged 78.9 percent for all groups. Of the 176,000 families in Brooklyn in 1980, married-couple families made up 47.8 percent, the lowest in all the boroughs of New York City. Of these married-couples families, 47 percent had two earners. The income gap in annual earnings between married-couple and female-headed families was enormous: $17,075 versus $7,172, respectively, with earnings of $6,141 for female-headed households with children under 18.

As in other urban areas, the structure of employment in Kings County has undergone significant change. Over the past two decades, in evidence of the trends discussed earlier in the chapter, the manufacturing sector in Kings County has declined as firms moved away to more attractive locations with lower costs of labor. Table 4.9 shows a sharp decline in the share of manufacturing employment and a doubling of the share of employment in services between 1972 and 1987. Overall, total employment declined by almost 100,000. It is important to note that not all who live in Kings County work there. Census data

Table 4.8

Male/Female Ratio of Jamaican Immigrants in 1980, by Age

Age Group	Female	Male	Males per 100 Females
20–24	11,500	9,200	80.0
25–29	10,100	8,800	87.1
30–34	11,300	8,700	77.0
35–39	11,200	8,600	76.8
40–44	9,700	7,300	75.3
45–54	14,500	11,000	75.9
55–64	9,800	7,900	80.6
TOTAL	78,100	61,500	Av.: 78.9

Source: U.S. Bureau of the Census, *Foreign-born Population in the United States: 1980 Census of the Population* (Washington, D.C.: Microfiche Technical Documentation, 1985).

Table 4.9

Distribution of Employment by Industry, Kings County, New York, 1972, 1987

Industry	1972	1987
Agriculture	0.05%	0.1 %
Mining	—	0.02
Construction	3.6	5.1
Manufacturing	35.8	20.5
Transportation	10.3	6.4
Wholesale trade	6.5	7.3
Retail trade	17.9	17.4
Services	19.4	37.0
TOTAL	477,420	379,221

Sources: U.S. Bureau of the Census, *County Business Patterns, New York: 1972* and *1987* (Washington, D.C.: U.S. Government Printing Office, 1974, 1989).

for 1980 show that 44.7 percent of those in the Brooklyn labor force worked outside their area of residence and took an average of 44.2 minutes to get to work, mostly by public transportation. This could place them in Manhattan, in some other borough, or even in New Jersey.

At the time of the 1980 U.S. Census, blacks represented 28.8 percent of Kings County employment. Table 4.10 shows that their employment was heavily concentrated in the technical, sales, administrative support, and service occupations.

Kasinitz observes that the relative prosperity of West Indians in New York is due more to their concentration in wage employment than to entrepreneurial activity (Kasinitz 1988, 187). Because West Indian immigrants in the decades before the 1960s had fewer job options, the incentive to start their own businesses was much greater. The typical small retail business, predominant in the early stages of the development of immigrant groups, is primarily a first-generation activity. As immigrant groups develop over time, the character of the business generally changes, requiring a higher level of sophistication. For example, it may evolve from a corner grocery store to a supermarket. As succeeding generations of West Indians acquire professional skills by investing in education, the path of success tends to move from the corner grocery to such places as the office, the classroom, or the laboratory.

Table 4.10

Percentage Distribution of Black Employment among Occupations, Kings County, New York, 1980

Occupations	% Employed
Managerial and professional specialty	13.8
Tech., sales, and admin. support	36.6[a]
Service occupations	24.2
Farming, forestry, and fishing	0.1
Precision prod., craft, and repair	7.5
Operators, fabricators, and laborers	17.5

Source: Bureau of the Census, *Census of Population, 1980: General Social and Economic Characteristics, New York,* PC80-1-C34 (Washington, D.C., U.S. Government Printing Office, 1983).
[a]Of this category, administrative support and clerical occupations account for 28.9 percent of black employment.

five

Temporary Migration and Illegal Aliens

The most perilous work in America is the harvest by hand of sugarcane in south Florida. It is performed by men from the West Indies who live in barracks on the sugar plantations. The majority come from Jamaica, but they also come from Barbados, St. Vincent, St. Lucia, and Dominica. The white people call them off-shore workers, offshores, H-2 workers (after the government program overseeing their use), H-2s, hand cutters, or simply—and most often—Jamaicans.

—Alec Wilkinson, "Big Sugar," New Yorker, 17 July 1989

While the majority of the Caribbean immigrants living permanently in the United States find employment in the service sector of their destination economies, temporary migrants work exclusively in agriculture. Most of these workers are from Jamaica. (See table 5.1.) They cut sugar cane on the plantations around the southern shore of Florida's Lake Okeechobee and pick apples along the East Coast.

The Florida sugar industry began importing workers from the West Indies in 1943, under the temporary work visa provision of the 1917 Immigration Act, to replace southern blacks who had moved north to work in war-related industries. In the post-war period, both the Mexican bracero program and the West Indies temporary worker program were authorized under section H-2 of the 1952 Immigration and Nationality Act. The bracero program—the result of a 1942 agreement between Mexico and the United States that allowed temporary workers from Mexico to work in the southwestern U.S. agricultural industry—was by far the larger of the two. In the 1960s, it came under attack by organized labor and was terminated by President Lyndon Johnson in 1964. McCoy and Wood attribute the survival of the West Indies farm worker program to its "low visibility" and "separate identity" (McCoy and Wood 1982, 6).

Although the farm worker program began in 1943, the Florida sugar industry's connection with the West Indies has been significantly influenced by events occurring since then. The expansion of the industry since 1961 can be attributed to the closing of the U.S. market to Cuban sugar. The industry has also benefitted from the entry of Cuban capital (McCoy and Wood 1982, 3). One sugar producer, Gulf and Western, the second largest sugar firm in Florida, sold its interest to a family from Cuba named Fajul (Wilkinson 1989, 66).

Table 5.1

West Indian Farm Workers Recruited, 1982–1989

Year	Jamaica	St. Lucia	Dominica	St. Vincent	Barbados	Grenada
1982	10,278	485	100	483	483	—
1983	9,926	504	98	505	498	—
1984	10,172	502	100	502	501	—
1985	10,880	502	129	470	490	25
1986	10,753	596	100	656	526	25
1987	11,401	562	100	552	416	25
1988	12,584	564	100	550	321	25
1989	12,597	580	110	620	263	25

Source: West Indies Central Labour Organization, Washington, D.C.

The Economics of Farm Worker Supply

The supply of farm workers to the United States is a function of the low wage rates and the high rates of unemployment in the Caribbean. The demand for them is a function of the inability of U.S. employers to attract native-born workers at prevailing wage rates. For rural Jamaican workers, these wage rates are highly attractive. And over the past 10 years they have been made even more so by the sharp devaluations of the Jamaican dollar.

The great majority of the temporary agricultural workers are recruited from the ranks of the agricultural labor force in Jamaica, particularly among peasant farmers. In their survey, McCoy and Wood found that the principal occupation of 64 percent of the recruited workers was farm-related work (McCoy and Wood 1982, 28). It is therefore useful to look at the structure of employment in Jamaica's agriculture. Agriculture is still the largest employer in Jamaica, and it has the lowest unemployment rate of all the economic sectors, averaging one-quarter of the national rate, which hovered around 25 percent during the 1980s. This low unemployment rate is misleading, however, because it masks the fact that most of those who are so employed are listed as being in "self-employed and independent occupations." In other words, they are small farmers, most of whom devote only part of their time to farming, partly because of the seasonality of agricultural production and partly because many farms are too small to occupy a farmer fully throughout the year.

Output per worker in agriculture is the lowest of all the economic sectors in Jamaica. So even if there was full employment in that sector, the withdrawal of some workers for export to America would have a negligible impact on total agricultural output. David Griffith argues that although "seasonal labor requirements of Jamaican peasant farming systems demand that most of the labor will

Table 5.2

Total Cash Flow from Jamaican Farm Workers in the United States, 1973–1982 (Millions of U.S.$)

Year	Workers Recruited	Mandatory Remittances[a]	Voluntary Remittances[b]	Cash Brought Back[c]	Total Cash Flow
1973	10,743	$5.870	$5.615	$6.879	$18.364
1974	10,051	5.493	5.254	6.436	17.183
1975	10,262	5.608	5.364	6.571	17.543
1976	8,656	4.730	4.525	6.125	14.380
1977	10,031	5.069	4.849	5.940	15.858
1978	10,031	5.482	5.243	6.423	17.148
1979	8,787	4.802	4.593	5.626	15.021
1980	10,128	5.535	5.294	6.485	17.314
1982	10,278	5.617	5.372	6.581	17.570

Sources: Government of Jamaica, *Statistical Yearbook of Jamaica* (Kingston: Department of Statistics, 1984); *Statistical Abstract 1977* (Kingston: Department of Statistics, 1977).
[a]Figures are based on the per capita U.S. dollar remittance in 1976, the last year for which data were available.
[b]Based on an estimate by Charles Wood (1982)) of US$518 remitted through the postal service by each farm worker in 1982.
[c]Based on an estimate by David Griffith (1986, 890) that 51 percent of gross after mandatory and voluntary remittances is spent on consumer goods and on board. Therefore, cash brought back represents the remaining 49 percent.

be required while the farm workers are abroad," the indirect effect of money remitted by farm workers to their wives and common law spouses back home is to help keep agricultural output stable not only on the farms of the migrants but also on the farms of the day laborers hired by the spouses (Griffith 1986, 890–91). McCoy and Wood suggest that most of the work on the farm is done by the extended family of the absent farm worker and only a relatively small amount by hired labor (McCoy and Wood 1986, 39).

The withdrawal of workers from domestic agriculture has long been a part of the rural-urban migration phenomenon. The inability of the major urban centers to absorb all of them has led to the formation of a large informal economy of self-employed people. In effect, what has occurred is the transfer of workers from one largely low-wage, self-employed sector to another. If against this background, farm work in the United States is presented as an option for potential rural-urban migrants, the choice would be obvious.

Farm Worker Remittances

The gains from farm work in the United States exceed any loss in income in agriculture or in the informal urban economy. Table 5.2 shows the estimated net gain as the difference between the total cash flow from Jamaican farm workers in the United States and the calculated value of agricultural output foregone. Agricultural output foregone is based on the assumption that all farm workers were employed in agriculture before they left. Under the farm worker's contract, 23 percent of gross earnings must be deposited in an interest-free savings account in the home country. This ensures a minimum inflow of foreign exchange from farm work. In 1976, for example, this was J(Jamaican)$4.3 million. Gross farm worker earnings that year, therefore, were J$18.7 million. Since 8,656 workers were recruited that year, gross earnings per farm worker were J$2,160, or US$2,376 at the prevailing exchange rate of J$.9091 to the U.S. dollar. In the absence of earnings data after 1976, we assume that gross U.S dollar earnings per farm worker remained the same in subsequent years. This is a reasonable assumption since farm worker wage rates and productivity remained generally stable. This means that in 1982, when 10,278 Jamaican farm workers were recruited, their gross earnings were US$24.4 million.

Wood estimates that in 1982 each farm worker remitted US$518 through the postal service (Wood 1982, 8). This would represent approximately 22 percent of gross earnings (US$518 divided by US$2,376). We assume, therefore, that over the period covered in table 5.2, voluntary remittances represented 22 percent of gross earnings. This means that both mandatory and voluntary remittances would add up to 45 percent of gross earnings. The remaining 55 percent gross earnings in 1982 would be US$13.4 million. Griffith estimates that 51 percent is spent on consumer goods and board (Griffith 1986, 890). This would amount to US$6.8 million, leaving US$6.6 million, or US$642 per farm worker, to take home. Thus the total amount of earnings flowing to Jamaica in 1982 (the mandatory and voluntary flow of US$11 million plus cash taken home of US$6.6 million) would be equal to US$17.57 million, compared with the value of agricultural output foregone of US$8.839 million (shown in table 5.3), yielding a net gain of US$8.731 million. If the farm workers were not employed before they left home, the value of agricultural output foregone would be zero and the net gain would be equal to the total cash flow. No matter how it is viewed, the farm worker program is beneficial to the farm workers and their families, as well as to the balance of payments of Jamaica.

The workers are recruited around October for a period generally lasting up to six months. As long as they are at work in the United States, a steady flow of remittances goes to their households. While these remittances are an important source of foreign exchange for the home country, they may also be viewed as the price the worker is paid for long periods of separation from his family. Important family celebrations such as Christmas and Easter are often missed. Some families disintegrate when the farm workers are away, but long separations have been an integral part of the family life of migrant Caribbean workers. In the early part of this century, they traveled in large numbers without their families to build the Panama canal.

Table 5.3

Net Gain from Jamaican Farm Workers in the United States, 1973–1982 (Millions of U.S.$)

Year	Total Cash Flow	Agric. Output Foregone[a]	Net Gain
1973	$18.364	$7.249	$11.118
1974	17.183	7.547	9.636
1975	17.543	10.160	7.293
1976	15.380	9.021	6.359
1977	15.858	11.091	4.767
1978	17.148	6.836	10.312
1979	15.021	6.583	8.438
1980	17.314	8.412	8.902
1982	17.570	8.839	8.731

Sources: Government of Jamaica, The Labour Force, 1974, 1985 (Kingston: Department of Statistics, 1975, 1986); National Income and Product, 1975 (Kingston: Department of Statistics, 1976).

[a]The per capita gross domestic product at current prices of employed workers in the Jamaican agricultural sector multiplied by the number of farm workers recruited for work in the United States. Converted into U.S. dollars at prevailing exchange rates.

Combining Cheap Labor with American Capital

The combination of cheap Caribbean labor with American capital has been a common post–World War II phenomenon. While labor-intensive manufacturing has been able to move offshore, agriculture cannot; it must import its cheap labor. In south Florida, the sugar cane fields on the south shore of Lake Okeechobee are for the most part located in soil so soft it's called muck. This makes the use of mechanized equipment for reaping impractical, because the equipment would pull the sugar cane roots from the soil, thereby eliminating future crops, which grow from the roots, known as ratoon. As a consequence, the sugar industry is dependent on cheap labor from the Caribbean.

When manufacturing capital goes offshore in search of cheap labor, the manufacturer is usually offered tax concessions by the host country. Some of these labor-intensive industries are allowed to operate in free-trade zones, where they pay no local income taxes. Analogously, when imported workers go to work with American capital in the Florida sugar industry, they too operate in a kind of implicit free-trade zone. They pay no U.S. income taxes, and they are forbidden to sell their labor to employers outside the sugar industry in the same way that free-trade-zone manufacturing firms are forbidden to sell their products domestically.

While these two situations are analogous in many respects, the analogy should not be stretched too far. The fact is that imported workers are captive in a way that offshore capital is not. A worker whose performance is deemed unsatisfactory or who is viewed as troublesome may be summarily fired and deported. And if he has not completed 50 percent of his time under the contract, he would have to pay his own fare back home. This threat of deportation keeps the workers in line and forces them to work hard to meet their daily performance quotas. U.S. labor unions have often challenged this arrangement in court on the grounds that employers prefer to hire cheap and docile foreign labor even when local labor is available. Employers, however, have consistently beat back these challenges with the argument that local workers are neither as reliable nor as productive as foreign ones, especially the Jamaicans, who compose 80 percent of all West Indian farm workers.

The farm worker program for the sugar industry is managed by the Florida Fruit and Vegetable Association (FFVA), and the interests of West Indian workers are represented by the West Indies Central Labour Organization (WICLO), which has a permanent office in Washington, D.C. The governing council of WICLO is the Regional Labour Board, which is made up of officials from the Jamaican government and one Jamaican labor union, as well as representatives of the governments from other participating countries. The contract for farm workers is renegotiated each year between the Regional Labour Board and industry representatives. The U.S. Sugar Corporation, the largest of the sugar firms, recruits its workers directly (McCoy and Wood 1982, 9).

The preference for West Indian workers creates a kind of bilateral monopoly in which there is one supplier—the West Indies—and one employer—the Florida sugar industry. In such a situation, the employer would theoretically want to pay a wage that is below the value of the additional output produced by an additional hour's work (the value of the marginal product), while the monopoly labor supplier would want a wage equal to the value of the marginal product. Negotiation between the two would produce a compromise wage reflecting the relative power of the negotiators. In the actual situation, the power of the sugar industry is far greater than that of the supplier of labor, largely because there is an unlimited number of West Indians willing to cut sugar cane in Florida at American wage rates. The wage rate for farm workers is set slightly above the U.S. minimum wage by the U.S. Department of Labor (DOL), which must approve the employers' request for imported labor. The DOL establishes what is called "the adverse wage rate," which is a "guaranteed hourly wage which should not only attract domestic workers but also, failing to do so, not adversely affect the wages of U.S. workers in related activities (i.e., agricultural workers)" (McCoy and Wood 1982, 7). Although this rate is slightly above the U.S. minimum, it is several times higher than wage rates in Jamaica.

U.S. Sugar—A Protected Industry

There is a certain irony when sugar-exporting Caribbean countries export workers to work in the United States sugar industry, which often lobbies for import tariffs and quotas on sugar from the Caribbean. When a subsidized U.S. industry operates in a protected market and imports cheap labor from abroad, it cannot help but be profitable. As McCoy and Wood put it: "Perhaps even more than other agricultural commodities in the U.S., the profitability of sugar is closely linked to the policies of the federal government" (McCoy and Wood 1982, 4).

The history of federal price supports for the sugar industry began with the Sugar Act of 1934, which established a "price objective" for sugar. This price support program remained in force until 1974, when it was repealed. For two years after that sugar prices were determined by the international market. In 1977, the current loan rate system was established. It guarantees growers a certain price per pound for sugar and allows them to take out loans to cover planting and cultivating costs, repayable with interest after the harvest. According to the *Washington Post*, "the industry received a price support of 13.5 cents [per pound] in 1977 and got it renewed at 16.75 cents in 1981 and 18 cents in 1985, the current price" (Gugliotta 1990, A4). In 1985, the loan rate system was modified to include a "no cost provision." Under this provision, the U.S. Department of Agriculture supports the 18-cent-a-pound price by carefully adjusting imports and exports to make sure there is no surplus sugar for the government to buy (Gugliotta 1990, A4). By way of comparison with the 18-cent-a-pound subsidized price, in 1985 Jamaica exported sugar at 14.6 cents per pound, and in the first half of 1990, sugar averaged 11.4 cents per pound on the New York Coffee, Sugar, and Cocoa Exchange.

Faced with this unfair competition in the U.S. sugar market, Caribbean countries can justify their export of labor as a way of recovering the foreign exchange lost to U.S. quotas and tariffs. In 1976, for example, mandatory farm worker remittances were equivalent to 28 percent of the value of Jamaica's sugar exports to the United States, and total remittances were equivalent to 66 percent.

Temporary Visitors

Despite the tight economic conditions in the 1980s, there was a rise in the number of people from the Caribbean who visited the United States for pleasure; an annual average of 134,000 nonimmigrants came from Jamaica alone between 1981 and 1986. (See table 5.4.) Of these, 64 percent were listed by the Immigration and Naturalization Service (INS) as "temporary visitors for pleasure." In other words, they were tourists. Many writers tend to treat these tourists as potential illegal aliens. Harris Miller, for example, implies that their propensity to violate their temporary visas is high: "Because the [INS] is aware of so many visa abusers from Caribbean nations, they scan visa applicants from these countries carefully" (Miller 1985, 356). While it is true that most of the illegal aliens from the Caribbean in the United States are people who violated the conditions of their temporary visas by seeking employment, their propensity to violate their visas is in fact quite low. Over the period 1963 to 1986, for example, an average of 1.5 percent of the temporary visitors from Jamaica violated the conditions of their visas (Palmer 1990, 172).

What is ignored is their beneficial impact on the U.S. economy. To the extent that these Caribbean tourists spend money on hotel accommodation and consumer goods, the localities in which they spend it clearly benefit. Even if some of these tourists stay with relatives and friends, many of them travel on American airlines and purchase goods and services during their visit. The average amount spent could easily add up to $500 per person. At that rate, Jamaican tourists, who compose 64 percent of all nonimmigrants from Jamaica (the rest

Table 5.4

Nonimmigrants from the Caribbean Admitted to the United States, 1976-1986

Year	Jamaica	Trinidad and Tobago	Barbados	Guyana
1976[a]	136, 930	47, 051	14, 062	13, 570
1977[a]	127, 990	51, 976	19, 111	14, 933
1978[a]	142, 538	61, 690	17, 959	18, 228
1979[a]	98, 466	41, 948	10, 706	12, 053
1981	111, 572	81, 051	19, 240	11, 271
1982	136, 070	104, 326	22, 321	12, 991
1983	160, 949	119, 048	24, 953	19, 089
1984	117, 493	98, 282	21, 925	17, 889
1985	128, 929	89, 052	22, 339	14, 289
1986	149, 376	75, 498	23, 568	18, 139

Sources: Immigration and Naturalization Service, Annual Reports.
Note: Data for 1976-79 based on country of birth; data for 1981-82 based on country of last permanent residence; data for 1983-86 based on country of citizenship.
[a] Includes returning resident aliens.

of whom are businesspeople, diplomats, and international civil servants), would have spent an average of $43 million annually between 1981 and 1986. To the extent that they traveled on the national airline of their country, however, some of this money would be retained at home.

Students

Table 5.5 shows that the major increases in the number of students from the English-speaking Caribbean between 1976 and 1986 came from the more prosperous economies. The number from Trinidad and Tobago, for example, increased almost four-fold while that from Barbados doubled. For Jamaica the numbers remained relatively stable, and for Guyana they declined. These two economies experienced the sharpest decline in their exchange rates over that period. What is striking in the data is that Trinidad and Tobago sent 20 percent more students to the United States than Jamaica and 10 times as many as Guyana, even though its population is half that of Jamaica and only slightly larger than that of Guyana. The explanation for this lies in the oil-driven prosperity of Trinidad and Tobago, which generated large amounts of foreign reserves and a strong currency up until 1986. The rise in oil prices in the 1970s that helped Trinidad and Tobago was accompanied by falling world market

Table 5.5

Caribbean Students Admitted to the United States, 1976–1986

Year	Jamaica	Trin. and Tob.	Guyana	Barbados	Dom. Rep.
1976	1,867	683	420	129	1,578
1977	2,183	701	425	204	1,222
1978	2,090	839	396	155	1,202
1979	1,404	521	201	149	562
1981	1,855	1,518	281	249	1,022
1982	2,074	1,852	248	276	903
1983	2,928	2,915	288	371	1,033
1984	1,715	2,348	193	290	708
1985	1,821	3,205	197	364	746
1986	1,850	2,883	268	408	624

Source: U.S. Immigration and Naturalization Service, Statistical Division, Washington, D.C., 1990.

prices for aluminum, which together had a negative impact on bauxite-producing Jamaica and Guyana. Consequently, the value of their currencies fell precipitously. While the substantial amount of U.S. aid that poured into Jamaica under the Edward Seaga regime of the 1980s may have helped to stabilize the flow of Jamaican students to the United States, Guyana fared less well and the number of its students declined sharply.

The falling value of the currencies of their home countries has raised the price of higher education in America for Caribbean students beyond the normal price increases faced by American students. This has forced many foreign students from the Caribbean to supplement whatever support they receive from home by working. The employer sanctions of the Immigration Reform and Control Act (IRCA) of 1986 have made this more difficult. In the end, falling currency values at home and employer sanctions in the United States may combine to reduce the role of the United States as the major supplier of higher education to the Caribbean.

Illegal Aliens

Prior to the passage of the IRCA, the discussion of illegal migration in the literature was based largely on guesswork. Data gathered from the amnesty program of the IRCA has facilitated a more precise count of illegal aliens, although not by any means a comprehensive count, since those eligible for the program had to have resided continuously in the United States prior to 1 January 1982, and

Table 5.6

Caribbean Legalization Applications by Country of Citizenship and Type of Illegal Status as of 16 May 1990, Pre-1982 Illegals

Country	Total	Illegal Entry	% of Total	Violated Temp. Visa	% of Total	Other	% of Total
Caribbean	59,895	32,087	53.6	27,596	46.0	212	0.4
Antigua-Barbuda	1,373	336	24.5	1,034	75.3	3	0.3
Bahamas	2,178	429	19.7	1,731	79.5	18	0.8
Barbados	1,045	144	13.8	901	86.2	131	12.6
Dom. Rep.	18,285	15,789	86.3	2,477	13.5	19	0.2
Haiti	15,962	7,594	47.6	8,282	51.9	86	0.5
Jamaica	13,003	5,414	41.6	7,533	57.9	56	0.5
Trinidad and Tobago	3,093	723	23.3	2,357	76.2	13	0.5
Guyana	3,116	1,576	50.6	1,535	49.3	5	0.1
Others	1,840	82	4.5	1,746	94.9	12	0.7

Source: Statistical Division, U.S. Immigration and Naturalization Service, 1990.

those who were special agricultural workers had to have worked in qualifying perishable agriculture for at least 90 days between May 1985 and May 1986. Some illegal aliens were simply afraid to apply. As of 16 May 1990, 123,468 illegal aliens from the Caribbean had applied to legalize their status, 48.5 percent of whom had applied under the continuous residence requirement and the rest under the Special Agricultural Workers (SAW) program. (See tables 5.6 and 5.7.)

Illegal aliens may have entered the country legally but become illegal when they overstayed their temporary visas. Some illegal aliens may have entered the country with no documents at all, as in the case of Dominicans who enter Puerto Rico clandestinely and board a domestic flight to New York, or Mexicans who walk across the Rio Grande. Fifty-four percent of all pre-1982 applicants entered the United States illegally. Eighty-six percent of the Dominicans entered the country illegally, most of them through Puerto Rico. (See table 5.6.) Guyana and Haiti had the second (50.6 percent) and third (47.6 percent) largest shares of applicants who entered illegally. Most of the Haitians were boat people who arrived in great numbers in the early 1980s; under the Cuban-Haitian Adjustment Program of the IRCA, most were allowed to regularize their status. Half of all Caribbean applicants were special agricultural workers, with those from Haiti accounting for 69 percent of the total and 73 percent of all Haitian applicants, the highest share of any Caribbean country.

Table 5.7

Total Caribbean Legalization Applicants by Country of Citizenship and Type of Application as of 16 May 1990

Country	Total	Pre-1982 Illegals	Special Agric. Workers
Caribbean	123,468	59,895	63,573
Antigua-Barbuda	1,449	1,373	76
Bahamas	2,396	2,178	218
Barbados	1,176	1,045	131
Dom. Rep.	28,138	18,285	9,853
Haiti	59,968	15,962	44,006
Jamaica	19,232	13,003	6,229
Trin. and Tob.	5,427	3,093	2,334
Guyana	4,226	3,116	1,110
Others	1,455	1,840	384

Source: Statistical Division, U.S. Immigration and Naturalization Service, 1990.

Applicants from the English-speaking Caribbean were mostly pre-1982 illegals who had violated their nonimmigrant visas. The share of visa violators among the pre-1982 applicants ranged from 57.9 percent for Jamaica to 86.2 percent for Barbados. Of all the applicants—pre-1982 plus special agricultural workers—Haiti (48.5 percent) and the Dominican Republic (22.8 percent) accounted for the largest shares.

While these applicants for legalization provide a useful measure of illegal aliens in the United States, an accurate count would have to include those apprehended by the INS. Even though this figure would not be 100 percent accurate because not all the pre-1982 illegals may have applied for legalization, it would be far superior to the wild estimates thrown around prior to the amnesty program. Between 1963 and 1981, some 18,000 Jamaican aliens were apprehended and required to leave the country. If we add this number to the 13,000 pre-1982 applicants, we get a total of 31,000 illegal aliens who either entered illegally or violated the conditions of their nonimmigrant visas. While it is not certain that all of the applicants entered the country between 1963 and 1981, the probability that many entered before 1963 appears to be low, since those applicants would likely be among the 45–64 age group, which makes up only 9 percent of all pre-1982 applicants. These numbers suggest, therefore, that illegal migration from Jamaica prior to 1982 was considerably smaller than the estimates of hundreds of thousands that were circulating prior to the 1986 law. Even when the agricultural applicants and those illegal aliens who came after 1982 are included, illegal migration from Jamaica remains modest.

The Connecting Link

There is an important link between temporary workers, temporary visitors, and illegal aliens, quite aside from the potential for some temporary workers and visitors to become illegal aliens. What really ties these groups together is the level of economic development in the Caribbean. As economic development raises wage rates and widens the range of job opportunities at home, the incentive for workers to seek temporary employment in America is likely to decline, as will the propensity to want to stay in the country illegally. Economic development will also tend to increase the number of people able to visit the United States for pleasure. The net result is that economic development will replace temporary workers and illegal aliens with temporary visitors for pleasure. This would be mutually beneficial to the Caribbean and the United States. The standard of living in the Caribbean would be higher, and Caribbean visitors to the United States would spend more. This future was briefly demonstrated during the oil boom of the 1970s when Trinidadians routinely traveled to Miami to shop. The Trinidadian airline, British West Indian Airways, was likened to a flying shopping cart.

One implicit objective of the Caribbean Basin Economic Recovery Act of 1983 (more popularly known as the Caribbean Basin Initiative) was to reduce the flow of both legal and illegal migration from the Caribbean by removing trade barriers and encouraging the flow of private capital to the region. The success of this program has been limited, but its premise remains valid.

six

Gains from Immigration

P rior to World War II, when migration from the Caribbean was primarily a temporary movement of unskilled workers, the principal benefits to the migrants were their earnings from higher wage rates abroad. Migration did not provide opportunities for investment in education and training. And since the migrant did not bring his family with him, the education of the children abroad was not a consideration in the migration decision.

The character of migration changed significantly after the war, from a temporary movement of individual workers to a permanent movement of households. It also changed from a movement to other developing countries within the Caribbean basin to a movement to the developed countries of North America and Europe, where success in these industrial societies means upward mobility and where upward mobility requires investment in education. Since it usually takes more than one generation for an immigrant group to reach parity with the native-born population, a household's investment in the education of its children is of critical importance. Thus, it is argued that the big difference between the gains from migration before and after World War II is the extent to which the immigrants have been able to enhance their capacity to earn. The need to enhance the capacity to earn is dictated by the permanence of the migration as well as by the skill requirements of the host society.

This chapter looks at the gains from immigration for the immigrants and for the sending and receiving countries. The gains for the immigrants are defined in terms of the acquisition of professional and technical skills by young immigrants since their time of arrival, the gains for the receiving country as output produced and for the sending country as the money sent back by immigrants. In examining the acquisition of professional and technical skills by young immigrants, the focus is on those 10-to-19-year-old immigrants from Jamaica who arrived in the United States over the 1960–69 period and who by the census year 1980 were 30–39 years old.

Gains for the Immigrants

Of the 2,700 10–19-year-old male Jamaican immigrants who arrived in 1960–69, 21.4 percent were listed as being in professional specialty occupations in 1980. And of the 2,900 10–19-year-old females who arrived during the same period, the figure was 16.7 percent. Altogether, 19 percent of this group were in professional specialty occupations in 1980.

How would these young immigrants have fared had they remained in Jamaica? Jamaican data provide us with a reasonable answer. In 1960, there were 327,000 10–19 year-olds in the country. By 1979, when they had become 30–39 year-olds, there were 193,700 of them. In that same year, 37,700 people were listed as professionals with or without a degree or diploma. Assuming that the occupational distribution of the 30–39-year-old cohort is similar to that for the country's labor force in 1979, only 9.2 percent would have been classified as professional, technical, and kindred workers, a much smaller share than that of those who migrated. Even if we allow for the fact that the parents of those 10–19 year-olds who migrated had a higher share of professionals among them (11 percent for 1962–69) than did the Jamaican labor force as a whole, the wide gap between the educational achievement of the immigrants and those who remained behind must be attributed to greater access to education in the United States. The difference in the professional shares of the two groups represents the net human capital gain resulting from migration. It can be argued, therefore, that the opportunity cost of not migrating is the lost human capital potential and the income associated with it.

The net human capital gain from migration accrues entirely to the migrants and their new country. But since the majority of the 10–19 year-olds who migrated were not likely to have been in the Jamaican labor force, there would have been little or no loss in output in that country. They would, however, cease to consume private and public goods, theoretically making more of them available for those remaining behind. Since some of the immigrants would undoubtedly have become skilled professionals had they remained at home, their migration clearly represents a potential loss to the sending country. But this potential loss pales beside the potential gain in the form of higher living standards for the immigrants themselves.

Gains for the Sending and Receiving Countries

While at the micro level, migration is primarily about improving the economic condition of the immigrant household. At the macro level, both sending and receiving countries may also gain. R. Albert Berry and Ronald Soligo, in their seminal contribution to the economic theory of international migration, argue that although the immigrant does not own, at least initially, any of the physical capital he works with, he receives a wage equal to the value of his additional output (marginal product). The authors assume a competitive labor market. The profits made are shared by the native owners of capital, causing their average income to rise (Berry and Soligo 1969, 784). They conclude that if the immigrant workers do not share in the returns to capital (via dividends and interest, for example), the combined income of native owners of capital and workers will generally be higher because the total profits from capital would exceed whatever loss in income that might result from lowered wages. If the immigrant is able to capture the returns to capital, then both native owners and workers together would experience a net loss. But Julian Simon points out that "the average immigrant family's net contribution to the public coffers far outweighs the loss to natives through the capture of the returns to capital by the immigrants" (Simon 1989, 152).

Some immigrants bring large amounts of financial capital with them, as is the case with some wealthy immigrants from Hong Kong to Canada and Australia in recent times. These are obviously not typical immigrants. They are capitalists, in contrast with the majority of immigrants, who are workers. As capitalists, they create employment for other people, both natives and immigrants. And as immigrants, they capture the return from the capital they invest. But what if all their employees are immigrants? The Berry and Soligo model would suggest that the native population would not be better off. Indeed, the native population would be worse off if the immigrant workers lowered wage rates for native workers and the immigrant capitalist captured all the returns to capital. The immigrant capitalist and the immigrant workers would, of course, have to pay taxes, and by so doing help to pay for the use of public facilities. While this may be an extreme example in the case of large enterprises, it is not at all extreme when we look at small enterprises, especially those of the "mom and pop" kind such as grocery stores. These small enterprises typically employ only family members, who may be paid no formal wages. Thus, they don't create any employment for natives. The owners capture all the returns from their investment. The fact that they pay no formal wages means that they are hiring family members cheaply. As these businesses proliferate in a particular locality, they would have the effect of suppressing wage rates for natives who may want to work in similar jobs. It would appear, therefore, that the natives would experience a net loss. The gains of the immigrants would be the net loss of the natives. The validity of this argument would be undermined if the larger economy is growing vigorously and higher-wage job opportunities are opening elsewhere for natives. If this is not happening, the gains of the immigrants may be seen as coming at the expense of natives.

Yet how can this be when historically in America the success of immigrants has been viewed as a stimulant to the growth of the national economy? This is true as long as the gains for the immigrants more than offset the losses some natives may experience, causing the national wealth to grow. And the argument has always been that as the national wealth grows, the rest of the country will benefit through some multiplier effect. It is a version of the trickle-down theory that doesn't work very well today, when most of the new jobs created are in the low-wage service sector of the economy.

If we extend the Berry and Soligo analysis to the sending country, we could argue that if the emigrants did not have ownership rights to capital assets in their home country and if they worked in a perfectly competitive market where they were paid a wage equal to the value of their addition to total output, their migration would theoretically have the opposite effect on the income of the owners of capital in the sending country. For one thing, the wage rate of the remaining workers in the sending country would tend to rise and output would fall. The rise in wage rates and the fall in output together would reduce the returns to capital by more than the rise in wages, and, following the logic of Berry and Soligo, this would create a net loss for the sending country. The experience of Jamaica described in chapter 1 suggests that many firms had problems finding replacement workers during the surge of migration in the 1970s and that a lot of physical capital was left idle. The consequent reduction in output reduced the returns to capital and ultimately the standard of living of the people.

In the United States, the opposite occurred. The professional immigrants, especially the health professionals, filled positions in the hospitals at lower wages than would have been paid their American counterpart. Indeed, it was because wages were higher in other sectors of the U.S. economy that native workers migrated to those sectors, leaving immigrants to fill the vacuum in the lower-wage sectors. The immigrants helped to increase the production of services and the rate of return on capital.

As immigrants increase the rate of return to private capital, they put additional pressure on such existing public capital facilities as schools and hospitals. The greater crowding that they cause may reduce the quality of the service and may force local governments to invest in larger facilities. The question then is, who will pay for it? Assuming that the new facility is financed with borrowed money, as is normally the case, then the immigrant family will participate in the financing by paying taxes. Simon puts it this way: "with the taxes they pay, new dwellers help cover the service of this debt to an extent that the new dweller is not a burden on old dwellers in this respect. (Simon 1989, 153). If, on the other hand, as Simon argues, "all new construction were paid for on current account, immigrants would underpay for the structures they use, because they would be paying for only a part (on a per person basis equal to natives) of the new construction necessary for them, whereas all the cost of the new construction would be due only to them (causing increasing expenditure by the natives for the new construction) while not paying at all for the existing structures they would be using. And if the number of immigrants were small and there were little or no physical depreciation, natives would pay almost the entire cost of structures for immigrants" (Simon 1989, 153).

The problem gets complicated when the increasing immigrant density in a particular locality triggers an outward movement of middle-income native families. The net result is often a shrinking tax base and a loss of political clout—not necessarily because of an increase in the density of immigrants but possibly because of an increase in the density of low-income people. Elizabeth Bogen points to the deterioration of property values with the increase in the density of the Brooklyn population (Bogen 1987, 73). Since public schools in America are financed by property taxes, the ability of the city government to invest in new public facilities may be limited. Immigrant groups such as West Indians who keep their neighborhoods looking good and contribute in a positive way to the maintenance of property values may very well, on a per household basis, contribute a disproportionate share to the financing of the public schools in Brooklyn.

Remittances

If we look at the household as a unit of migration and if we argue that the primary motive for Caribbean migration is economic, then the economic improvement of the household must be the primary objective of migration. Remittances play an important role in this process.

The immigrant household seldom moves as a complete unit. Upon employment, the immigrant remits funds to the rest of the household in the country of origin. These remittances help finance the day-to-day living of those remaining behind as well as their eventual reunification with the immigrant household abroad. Thus, there is a circulating pattern to contemporary household migration from the Caribbean, with the flow of remittances providing an important link in this system. The return flow of remittances enhances the welfare of the household and facilitates its reunification. The underlying assumption here is that those who migrated did so with a view to settling abroad.

In cases where migration is temporary, remittances play the same important role of enhancing the welfare of the household. It is possible to envisage a situation in which the household makes a conscious decision to have some of its members go abroad for short intervals to improve household income. Some members of the household may work on ships or be part of a team of construction workers employed in different countries for short periods, or they may be farm workers. These workers typically have a high propensity to save, remitting large portions of their income to the rest of the household back home so that when they return they can live comfortably until it is time to travel again. The circularity of this pattern leads to the reunification of the household in the sending country.

Our focus, however, is on permanent migration and the ultimate reunification of the household in the receiving country. The implication here is that the process of migration for the household is not complete until reunification occurs. Reunification, then, is regarded here as a kind of equilibrium toward which migration tends. The existence of the flow of remittances in this context is a manifestation of the absence of this equilibrium. It is quite conceivable that disequilibrium may persist for a long time, especially when the household is defined as including the extended family: grandparents, aunts, cousins, etc.

The definition of "household" used in this volume is based on the nuclear family. Yet it is often difficult to separate the nuclear from the extended family, which plays an important role in taking care of children when members of the nuclear family migrate. And so remittances sent back to take care of the children and to prepare them for reunification with the household abroad also support members of the extended family. Sometimes members of the extended family are reunited with the nuclear family abroad to continue to care for young children. When this reunification takes place, the flow of remittances will cease. If there are members of the extended family left behind, who will not or cannot join the household abroad, then some remittances may continue to flow. Some remittances may also continue to flow into institutional savings in the sending country if the adult members abroad foresee the day when they might return home to retire. The essential point of this analysis is that the flow of remittances is a function of a temporarily divided household.

Most of these remittances are spent on consumption goods. Dawn Marshall argues that remittances have had little impact on the economic development of the Eastern Caribbean, although she concedes that at the level of the individual or the family they enhance material welfare (Marshall 1985, 91–116). The importance of remittances as a source of support for the families of migrants in St. Kitts and Nevis is underscored by Bonham Richardson: "Young people who go away are expected to provide financial support for family and friends left behind, and almost everyone left on the two islands depends, at least in part, upon the success of those, old and young, who have emigrated" (Richardson 1983, 47). Aside from the economic impact of remittances, there is a social impact not unlike that described by Jonathan Power in the case of Ireland, where remittances tend to undermine traditional family cooperation: "Families now feel more self-interested. The postal orders come from America or from Britain, and no one wants to tell anyone else how much they are getting. . . . Observers of the Irish agricultural scene point to a devastatingly destructive individualism that makes even the simplest co-operative venture—like building a road along a line of cottages—extremely difficult" (Powers 1979, 135).

In its *World Development Report 1984,* The World Bank argues that benefits from the emigration of unskilled workers in the form of remittances "are likely to be large" because the emigration of these workers "generally leads to no loss of production" (World Bank 1984, 101). It is a different matter, however, when it comes to the emigration of skilled workers. The cost to governments in the form of subsidies and lost taxes on immigrant income can be substantial (World Bank 1984, 102). Thus, against the background of the emigration of skilled workers, the net benefits from remittances are uncertain.

The idea of a tax on the earnings of immigrants in their new country to compensate for the subsidized education they received in the sending country has been discussed at length in the 1976 essay collection *Taxing the Brain Drain,* edited by J. N. Bhagwati and M. Partington. In one essay, authors Bhagwati and Dellalfar view such a tax "as a means of extracting from one's own professional manpower, part of the 'surplus' that is accruing to it via the act of migration: the LDC [less developed country] then sharing, as a reward for permitting migration to higher salary areas, in the differential return to migrant manpower" (Bhagwati and Partington 1976, 36). Based on an estimate of gross incomes of professional immigrants in the United States in 1969, Bhagwati and Dellalfar use a 10 percent tax rate to "arrive at the estimated 1969 tax collection figure of over \$62 million in the United States: a sum that is over a tenth of the net aid flow from the United States in 1971" (Bhagwati and Partington 1976, 37).

In its 1984 report, the World Bank, based on its assumption that emigrant professionals in each occupation in the United States received a salary equal to that of American workers in 1979, estimates that a 10 percent tax would yield \$600 million for sending countries, which was equivalent to 13 percent of official development assistance from the United States that year (World Bank 1984, 102). In the Jamaican case, as table 6.1 shows, remittances represented approximately 40 percent of official development assistance from all sources for 1982, 1983, and 1986. There is no assurance, however, that if such a tax were imposed, the governments receiving this money would use it to expand the productive capacity of the economy. But beyond this, the singling out of immigrants for special tax treatment, especially those in the United States, is fraught with constitutional problems. For the foreseeable future, therefore, voluntary remittances will have to be regarded as the return on society's investment in migrant human capital stock.

It will be up to the respective governments of sending countries to devise ways to induce these remittances into productive investments that will later reduce their countries' dependence on them. Pastor and Rogers propose the establishment of national remittance banks that would earmark the funds for economic development (Pastor and Rogers 1985, 321–42). But the nationalization of private remittances may operate as a disincentive to future flows if those abroad become disenchanted with government policies at home. Rubenstein goes so far as to suggest that "remittances, and perhaps the entire migratory

Table 6.1

Remittances from Abroad: Jamaica, 1970, 1982, 1983, 1986
(Millions of U.S.$)

Year	Remittances	Net Priv. Direct Investment	Merch. Exports	Official Development Assistance (ODA)	Remittances as % of ODA
1970	$29.0	$161.0	$—	$—	—
1982	75.0	(16.0)	726	180	41.7
1983	42.0	(19.0)	726	181	23.2
1986	96.0	2.0	586	177	54.3
					Av: 39.9

Sources: World Bank, *World Development Report, 1984; 1985; 1988* (New York: Oxford University Press, 1984; 1985; 1988).

system as presently constituted, are detrimental to the long-term prospects for economic improvement in most of the region's societies" (Rubenstein 1982, 260).

Jamaica has one of the highest emigration rates in the world, and the remittances from its expatriates are regarded as an important source of foreign exchange. It is therefore a useful example to study to assess the beneficial effects of remittances. When compared with the flow of net direct private investment or the value of merchandise exports, the flow of remittances is a major source of foreign exchange. The problem, however, with these comparisons is that these sources of foreign exchange do not have the same impact on the economy. In general, remittances are more likely to be used for consumption rather than for capital formation.

A small share of the remittances is invested in housing and in small businesses. But housing cannot be considered productive investment even though it generates a one-time demand for housing materials and furnishings. In a survey of some 200 return migrants to Jamaica, roughly one third depended on the savings they accumulated abroad to finance their small businesses. The authors concluded that for small businesses, "migration plays a significant role as the single largest source of capital formation" (Chevannes and Ricketts 1993, 37). Yet the connection between these small businesses and the economic development of the country is tenuous at best. Most of these businesses are in wholesale and retail and certain specialty services, and they employ few workers. Furthermore, they have an extremely high rate of failure.

The government of Jamaica has taken steps to induce a greater inflow of funds from abroad, including funds from Jamaican expatriates, by removing all controls on the exchange rate and the movement of foreign exchange into and out of the country. It now allows Jamaican nationals abroad to hold U.S. dollar accounts in Jamaican banks, with the freedom to withdraw U.S. dollars when they wish. This, combined with interest rates that rose as high as 40 percent, has induced a substantial increase in the inflow of funds from Jamaican nationals. These funds are far more likely to finance investments than the remittances normally sent to households.

Ultimately, all these dollar remittances will be spent on imports from the United States, a large part of which will be consumption goods because of the high import content in consumption in Jamaica. Thus the remittances sent back to support members of the household in the sending country ultimately wind up back in the United States, as they are used to purchase U.S. goods. Immigrant remittances are therefore delayed expenditures on goods and services from the United States. In this sense, immigration into the United States has a positive relationship with the export of goods and services from the United States. The more U.S. dollars that are remitted to sending countries, the more U.S. exports to these countries grow. The extent to which these exports will contribute to the economic development of the immigrant-sending countries will depend on the share of capital goods involved.

In the final analysis, the flow of remittances depends on the performance of the host country economy. A rapidly growing economy will provide greater opportunities for full-time work and therefore higher incomes for each immigrant household. Remittances, however, are not the only source of repatriated funds from immigrants.

In addition to monetary remittances, there are remittances in kind. Aside from occurrences of disaster, such as a hurricane or a flood, expatriates send a regular flow of remittances in kind back home. Airport baggage claim areas are often clogged with barrels and boxes of merchandise sent or brought back by expatriates.

Expatriates as Tourists

Relatively low airfares allow large numbers of Caribbean immigrants to make frequent pilgrimages back to their home country. There have been no studies of the expenditure of this group as separate from tourist expenditures. In the case of Jamaica, which has a large stock of its population in the United States, the volume of spending on return visits is substantial. Although many of these return visitors may not stay in local hotels, many do use the national airline and purchase local goods and services and specialty items to bring back to the United States. In Trinidad and Tobago at carnival time, large numbers of Trinidadian expatriates return on the national airline. So the spending of expatriates as tourists, though undifferentiated from aggregate tourist spending, has become an increasingly important part of the flow of funds from immigrants. Expatriates also return for more serious purposes, some to conduct business and some to bury members of their family.

Some indication of the volume of Caribbean immigrants who return to their home countries annually is given by the data in table 6.2, which shows the number of resident aliens returning to the United States by country of birth for the period 1977–79. The average annual number returning from Jamaica was 46,837, from Trinidad and Tobago, 18,846, and from Barbados 4,024. As a percent of tourist arrivals in these countries in those years, they represented nearly 10 percent for Jamaica and for Trinidad and Tobago and less than 1 percent for

Table 6.2

Returning Resident Aliens by Country of Birth, 1976–1979

Year	Jamaica	Trinidad and Tobago	Barbados
1976	45,303	18,388	3,716
1977	46,836	19,137	4,402
1978	56,060	20,263	4,956
1979	39,150	17,595	3,023
Annual average	46,837	18,846	4,024

Sources: U.S. Department of Justice, Immigration and Naturalization Service, *Annual Reports, 1976; 1977; 1978;* and *1979* (Washington, D.C: U.S. Government Printing Office, 1976; 1977; 1978; 1979).

Table 6.3

Resident Aliens in the United States as a Percent of Tourist Arrivals in Country of Birth, 1977–1979

Year	Jamaica	Trinidad and Tobago	Barbados
1977	11.7	9.4	1.2
1978	10.5	9.7	1.1
1979	6.6	10.3	0.6
Annual average	9.6	9.8	0.96

Sources: U.S. Department of Justice, Immigration and Naturalization Service, *Annual Reports, 1977; 1978;* and *1979* (Washington, D.C.: U.S. Government Printing Office, 1976; 1977; 1978; 1979).

Barbados. (See table 6.3.) Although these data do not include Caribbean-born U.S. citizens returning to the United States, they strongly indicate that the expatriate as tourist is a far more significant phenomenon in Jamaica and Trinidad and Tobago than in Barbados.

A Summing Up

When we examine the flow of foreign exchange in the form of remittances and money spent by returning nationals, we are in fact examining the returns on previous migration. Migration, then, takes on the character of an investment that generates a stream of earnings. It is difficult to determine precisely the monetary value of this investment. Much of it will depend on the number of years of schooling the emigrant had in the sending country, whether at public or private expense. Whatever the source of the financing of this education, the cost can be considered a national investment. If the purpose of early education is to shape the cultural identity of the individual, then its cost involves more than a mere outlay of funds over a relatively small number of years; it involves the sacrifices and struggles of previous generations. When all of this is summed up, it represents the cost of acquiring a cultural heritage. No amount of remittance can cover this investment.

seven

Migration, Employment, and Trade

The argument that trade creates employment and reduces the willingness to migrate has had a powerful influence on U.S. policy toward the Caribbean. It was an important part of the thinking behind the Caribbean Economic Recovery Act of 1983, which provided unilateral, tariff-free access to a wide range of exports from Caribbean basin countries. While the logic of this argument makes sense, in practice it has been difficult to implement. For one thing, trade must create jobs at a rate greater than the growth of the labor force in order to reduce the rate of unemployment. For another, wages paid by those jobs should be high enough to reduce the wide disparity in wage rates between the United States and the Caribbean. Trade can accomplish this only if there is a massive infusion of investment into export industries. This makes investment the yeast in the trade and employment mix.

Inadequate investment has been a problem for Caribbean countries, especially since the early 1960s, when they began to achieve political independence. This problem is exemplified by a statement in Guyana's development plan for 1966–72: "Expansion of output in many fields requires a high level of investment per worker employed and since total investment funds available are limited, creation of sufficient new jobs is limited" (*Guyana Development Programme 1966–1972*, 11–12).

Throughout the Caribbean this difficulty has perpetuated economic structures that depend on a limited number of export products that are often vulnerable to price fluctuations in world markets. Given the narrow base of these economies, and the inability of trade to provide enough employment, migration has been an important option for many people. The large scale migration to the United States that began in the 1960s is the latest manifestation of this phenomenon in the long history of Caribbean search for economic opportunities abroad.

Unlike the movement to the United Kingdom in the 1950s, migration to the United States has been controlled by the social objective of reuniting families and the economic objective of providing needed skills for the U.S. labor market. *The President's Comprehensive Triennial Report on Immigration, 1989* affirms the view of the Caribbean as an adjacent labor market: "Caribbean migration to the United States has become a primary mechanism for integrating various parts of the region into a single yet differentiated market" (U.S. Department of Labor

Table 7.1

Occupational Distribution of Caribbean Migration to the United States, Totals for 1967–1976

Occupations	Jamaica	Trinidad	Guyana	Barbados	Total
Professional and technical	7.6%	6.7%	10.5%	8.6%	17,649
Farmers and farm managers	0.1	0.0	0.1	0.0	266
Managers, officials, and proprietors	1.3	1.4	2.0	1.3	3,304
Clerical and kindred	6.5	7.2	9.7	7.2	16,112
Sales workers	0.8	0.8	0.9	1.1	1,937
Craftsmen, foremen, and kindred	8.5	9.1	7.1	9.2	19,601
Operatives and kindred	6.7	5.8	5.1	6.6	14,409
Private household	17.7	11.8	7.1	17.2	34,519
Service, except private household	4.1	4.4	3.8	6.0	9,869
Farm laborers and foremen	0.7	0.1	0.2	0.4	1,146
Laborers, except farm and mine	1.0	0.8	0.5	1.5	2,149
Housewives, children, and others	44.8	51.8	52.9	40.7	107,756
TOTAL	130,404	59,728	22,172	16,413	228,717

Sources: U.S. Immigration and Naturalization Service, *Annual Reports* (Washington, D.C., U.S. Government Printing Office, 1967–76).

1989, 8–9). The occupational distribution of English-speaking Caribbean immigrants to the United States for the decade 1967–76 is shown in table 7.1.

The Caribbean's role as a supplier of labor to the United States has its benefits and costs. On the one hand, it gives many workers an opportunity to improve their standard of living and to remit funds back to their home countries; on the other, it allows the United States to siphon off skilled workers from the region. This last point needs some elaboration, because the loss of skilled workers is not obvious from the data in table 7.1. In the table, three categories of immigrants account for two thirds of the migration: housewives, children, and others; clerical and kindred workers; and private household workers. These groups are generally regarded as having low levels of skills. To illustrate the significance of the loss of skilled workers, we focus on the migration of professional and technical workers (PT) from Jamaica. This group accounted for roughly 8 percent of the migrants in table 7.1. Between 1962 and 1972, official statistics show that the number of PT workers in the Jamaican labor force grew from 31,093 to 45,501, an increment of 14,408. Over the same period, 10,349 PT workers emigrated. If the growth of PT workers in the Jamaican labor force is considered to be net of migration, then the gross increase in that category would be equal to those who emigrated (10,349) plus those who remained (14,408), a total of 24,757. This means that 42 percent of the gross increase in PT workers emigrated—a high rate of emigration for any country, let alone a small developing one. Even if we allow for the fact that some of these workers received their education and training in the United States before they became immigrants, it is difficult to avoid the conclusion that the return to investment in education and training in Jamaica and other Caribbean countries is significantly reduced by migration.

If trade has not been able to reduce unemployment, neither has migration. The extent to which unemployment in the Caribbean is reduced by migration to the United States is negligible because those who migrate are either employed or are not in the labor force. Those not in the labor force include housewives and dependent children. (See table 7.1). Because unemployment is usually defined to include only those who are actively seeking work, the migration of housewives and children does not reduce the official unemployment figures.

The Constraints on Local Wage Rates

The principal incentives for employed people to migrate are higher wage rates and better working conditions. The attractiveness of higher wage rates abroad is reinforced by the constraints on wage growth at home. One such constraint is the persistence of a high rate of unemployment, especially in the lower-skilled occupations. Here, the existence of an excess supply of workers restrains the growth of wage rates. But wage rates are also constrained by world prices and the monopolistic structure of domestic industry. Because most Caribbean exports represent a relatively small share of world supply, they are subject to the behavior of world market prices. And because generally wages are influenced by the value of the worker's output, world market prices impose a constraint on the growth of wages. This is particularly true of agricultural and mineral exports for which world supply is plentiful. Further, because a handful of firms account for most of the employment in Caribbean export industries and face no serious competition for labor from other domestic employers, they are in a powerful position to control wages. Thus, the growth of wages for workers in the domestic export industries is subject to three important constraints: the excess supply of workers at home; world market prices; and the monopolistic structure of the export industries.

Workers in the public sector and in those private industries that produce nontradable goods and services (that is, exclusively for the domestic market) also face wage constraints. Here, the constraint on wage growth is not the world market but the monopoly power of the employer. Because the government is the major employer in these countries, it has great power over wage rates. The same is true for those private industries in which there is a dominant employer.

The question arises as to the extent to which skilled workers are affected by these wage constraints. In the Caribbean, generally, there is a relative scarcity of skilled workers in a wide range of occupations. Consequently, they will not experience the same degree of wage constraint as unskilled workers who are in excess supply. Skilled workers do experience some constraints on wage growth owing to world prices and the monopolistic structure of local export industries, but these constraints are partially offset by the relative scarcity of skills. The result is a wide income gap between the skilled and the unskilled. Still, despite their relatively favorable position at home, skilled workers in the Caribbean know that the gap between their income and that of their counterparts in the United States is wide. It is this gap that often influences their decision to migrate.

No matter in what sector of the Caribbean economy a worker is employed, constraints on monetary wage growth will always be a factor in the migration decision. And for unskilled workers, those constraints may be reinforced by the migration of skilled workers. Given some ratio of skilled to unskilled workers in the workplace, the migration of skilled workers may create greater unemployment among the unskilled.

The Caribbean finds itself in a dilemma: low wages attract foreign investment in labor-intensive industries and drive out skilled labor. When wage growth is constrained, the willingness to migrate intensifies, but if wages are allowed to rise, the region loses its advantage as a location for labor intensive industries. This trade-off leads to a vicious cycle as the region becomes a repository for low wage industries. Better technology could break this cycle by increasing the productivity of domestic labor. But better technology would also displace labor, an undesirable prospect in a region with high unemployment rates. Even if some employment were traded off for higher productivity, there is no assurance that wages would rise in the export industries because foreign demand might not absorb the increase in output per worker. Furthermore, when earnings from the greater supply of exports are constrained by world prices, most of the benefits from increased productivity would be transferred to the foreign consumer and little to the local worker in the form of wage increases. This is usually the case for agricultural and mineral exports, the foreign demand for which is not sensitive to the growth of foreign income. Because foreign demand for manufactured exports is generally more responsive to foreign income growth, Caribbean workers in manufacturing are likely to reap greater benefits from increased productivity.

A Regional Common Market

A principal objective of the creation of a regional Caribbean market is to expand intraregional trade, with the hope that this would stimulate greater investment and employment. The Caribbean Community (CARICOM), which was moribund throughout the 1980s, was created in 1973 out of the Caribbean Free Trade Area (CARIFTA) as the framework for establishing a regional common market. Tariffs on trade among the members would ultimately be removed and a common external tariff imposed on goods entering the market from abroad.

The deterioration of the economies of two of the larger members of CARICOM (Jamaica and Guyana) in the 1970s and 1980s halted progress toward this objective as these governments were forced to focus on their own economic problems. But there were other obstacles as well, chief among them the failure to agree on what is an appropriate external tariff and the free movement of labor. The problem with the common external tariff is that individual member countries are not equally efficient in domestic production, so that a common external tariff that may be appropriate for an efficient (low cost) producer may not be appropriate for an inefficient (high cost) producer. The tariff may allow imports to undermine the industries of the inefficient country. In addition, because revenues from customs duties represent an important share of government revenues, some countries worry about setting the common external tariff too low.

The basic argument for the free movement of labor is that if capital moves freely within the region, labor should also be allowed to move freely to take advantage of job opportunities created by capital. Despite the movement of temporary workers among the islands, migration within the Caribbean is in general controlled tightly, as Trevor Hope observes: "Immigration restrictions are most severe against those trying to enter the islands from within the region, but everywhere they are highly restrictive" (Hope 1985, 251). While many recognize that labor mobility would expand the capacity of the region to produce and therefore to compete more effectively in world markets, some countries fear that they will be inundated with the unemployed workers from other member countries. Some tentative steps have recently been taken to allow freedom of movement for professional workers, especially those trained at the regional universities.

Migration and the Caribbean Basin Initiative

The enactment of the Caribbean Basin Initiative (BI) in 1983 dealt an unintentional blow to the importance of CARICOM as a vehicle for regional economic integration. Through its unilateral elimination of tariffs on a wide range of Caribbean exports, the CBI made the Caribbean economies more dependent on the United States. The CBI's explicit objective of creating greater employment in the region through expanded trade and investment, particularly in such nontraditional industries as winter vegetables, electronics, and garment manufacturing, has had only limited success. But its implicit objective of reducing migration to the United States has been even less successful, as the migration flow continued unabated. Table 7.2 shows that in the decade of 1979–88 migration to the United States from the four major English-speaking Caribbean countries was more than 50 percent higher than that for the decade of 1967–76. The importance of this objective is underscored by Robert Pastor: "In a sense, migration has become a link whereby the United States shares the consequences of instability and underdevelopment in the region, and as such, it has become a rationale for U.S. security policy" (Pastor 1985, 1).

In the years following the enactment of the CBI, the general problem of illegal migration attracted a great deal of political attention, leading the U.S. Congress in 1986 to legislate amnesty for illegal aliens under the Immigration Reform and Control Act. While the share of illegal aliens from the Caribbean in the U.S. national total was relatively small, the number of those who had entered the country legally and became illegal aliens by overstaying their visas had grown (Palmer 1990, 163–74). Despite the restriction imposed by the IRCA on the employment of illegal aliens, the prospect of improving their standard of

Table 7.2

West Indian Migration to the United States, 1967–1976 and 1979–1988

Country	1967–76	1979–88
Jamaica	130,404	202,953
Trin. and Tob.	59,728	37,778
Guyana	22,172	88,605
Barbados	16,413	19,249
TOTAL	228,717	348,585

Source: Statistical Division, Immigration and Naturalization Service, Washington, D.C.

living in the United States still motivates people to migrate illegally. The case of the Haitian boat people is an extreme example—and one that underscores the argument that the principal long-term solution to the problem of illegal immigration is to strengthen Caribbean economies through trade and investment.

The sharp rise in the world oil prices in the 1970s and the worldwide recession of 1980–82 devastated the non-oil-producing Caribbean economies, bringing their foreign trade into decline. This decline in foreign trade stimulated an increase in both legal and illegal migration. While some of this migration represented a flight from the socialism that was rapidly undermining capitalism in Jamaica, Grenada, and Guyana, most of it represented a flight in search of better economic opportunities.

The success of the CBI was predicated on a vigorous U.S. economy, which would generate a strong demand for Caribbean products. The inherent contradiction of the CBI lay in the fact that while a prosperous U.S. economy increases its demand for Caribbean goods and services, it also increases its demand for skilled Caribbean workers. And as a U.S. economy in recession reduces its demand for Caribbean goods and services, causing Caribbean employment and wage rates to fall, it also intensifies the propensity of Caribbean skilled workers to migrate. For even in the deepest post-war recession, unemployment rates are much lower and wage rates much higher in the United States. So both in prosperity and in recession, the U.S. economy tends to pull workers from the Caribbean.

Devaluation and Wage Rates

When the U.S. economy is in a recession, the Caribbean economies relapse into a virtual state of depression because of the declining market for their exports. A sustained decline of Caribbean exports creates a shortage of foreign exchange, which often leads to a devaluation of the currency vis-à-vis other international currencies. If the foreign exchange crisis is severe, the country will try to supplement its depleted foreign exchange reserves by borrowing from the International Monetary Fund (IMF). As a condition for making such loans, the IMF

Table 7.3

Caribbean Currencies per U.S. Dollar for Selected Years

Country	1970	1976	1980	1985	1987
Jamaica	0.83	0.90	1.78	5.48	5.50
Trin. and Tob.	2.00	2.40	2.40	2.45	3.60
Barbados	2.01	2.01	2.01	2.01	2.01
Guyana	2.00	2.55	2.55	4.25	9.75
Haiti	5.00	5.00	5.00	5.00	5.00
Dom. Rep.	1.00	1.00	1.00	2.94	4.96

Sources: International Monetary Fund, *International Financial Statistics* (Washington, D.C.: International Monetary Fund, 1977, 1986, 1988).

almost always requires a devaluation of the borrowing country's currency. Its rationale is that such devaluation will correct the imbalance between export earnings and the payments for imports by reducing the price of exports and increasing the price of imports. The outcome, of course, will depend on the sensitivity of both foreign and domestic importers to these changes in prices.

The devaluation of a Caribbean currency not only lowers the price of Caribbean exports, it also lowers the price of Caribbean labor to U.S. businesses and makes U.S. wage rates more attractive to potential emigrants. This is so because the Caribbean currency is worth less in terms of the U.S. dollar and therefore the wages of Caribbean workers fall relative to those of U.S. workers. This makes the behavior of the exchange rate in these small, foreign-trade-dependent economies an important indicator of the willingness to migrate. The Caribbean countries from which the largest flows of immigrants have come since 1965—Guyana, Jamaica, and the Dominican Republic—have all experienced sharp declines in their foreign exchange rates, especially in the 1980s, as table 7.3 shows.

Falling exchange rates trigger a counterflow of labor and capital, labor migrating abroad for higher wages and foreign capital flowing in to take advantage of cheaper labor. This process tends to keep wage rates low and to make it difficult for the Caribbean to build the critical mass of skilled workers needed to attract high-technology industries.

Yet low wage rates are essential to the pursuit of an export-led strategy by Caribbean countries. This strategy has focused on nontraditional industries, a principal feature of which is offshore textile and apparel production. These offshore operations are typically located in free trade zones, assembling cut fabric imported from parent firms in America into finished garments that are exported to America. The decision of the parent firm to locate its labor-intensive operation offshore is encouraged not only by low labor costs but also by concessions provided under sections 806 and 807 of the U.S. tariff schedule. Under these concessions, a tariff is imposed only on the value-added portion of the finished product when it enters the United States.

Table 7.4

A Comparison of Wage Income Generated by Jamaica's 807 Exports to the United States with Remittances from Migrants, 1980–1986 (Millions of U.S.$)

Year	Exports	Value-added[a]	Wage Income[b]	Migrants' Remittances
1980	13.2	3.6	2.4	49.4
1981	16.1	4.4	2.9	61.7
1982	11.0	3.0	2.0	74.2
1983	12.8	3.5	2.3	40.4
1984	23.2	6.4	4.3	25.0
1986	70.2	19.3	12.9	99.8[c]

Sources: U.S. International Trade Commission, *Emerging Textile Exporting Countries 1984* (Washington, D.C., 1985); World Bank, *The Caribbean: Export Preferences and Performance* (Washington, D.C., 1988); International Monetary Fund, *International Financial Statistics* (Washington, D.C., 1988); International Monetary Fund, *Balance of Payments Statistics,* vol. 38, part 1 (Washington, D.C., 1987).
[a]Based on World Bank data for 1986, which showed that 27.5 percent of the value of 807 exports from Jamaica was value-added.
[b]Based on U.S. International Trade Commission estimate that workers in the United States account for one third of the value added to apparel and that it takes twice as many workers in Jamaica to add the same value.
[c]For 1985.

Because the garment-assembly industry is heavily dependent on cheap labor, the government is forced to keep wage rates low. This is usually accomplished through an incomes policy that controls the rate of increase in wages or through an exchange rate policy. While the downward trend in the exchange rate since the 1970s is attributable to a deteriorating balance of payments, it has served the purpose of lowering the cost of labor to foreign investors considerably. This is dramatically illustrated in the Jamaican case. In 1990, when the Jamaican dollar was worth 14 U.S. cents, the average hourly wage (including fringe benefits) in the apparel industry was 98 U.S. cents; the following year, when the Jamaican dollar fell to 8 U.S. cents, the average hourly wage fell to 58 U.S. cents (U.S. International Trade Commission 1992, 23). The exchange rate, however, is a two-edged sword, for while it lowers the cost of labor to foreign investors, it creates inflation at home, thus reducing the real wage.

The main purpose of attracting these offshore operations is to generate foreign exchange with abundant cheap labor. Some two-thirds of the value added to the assembled garments is attributed to the cost of labor. Thus, in an indirect way, labor is exported insofar as it is embodied in the assembled garments. But the indirect export of labor is not the only source of foreign exchange; the direct export of labor by individuals in the form of migration is as well. Table 7.4

compares the wage income generated by section 807 apparel exports with the remittances of migrants in the first half of the 1980s. Remittances were 8–20 times wage income. And even though the value of Jamaica's apparel exports to the United States has almost quadrupled since 1986, the wage income generated is still less than the remittances of migrants. If the generation of foreign exchange is the primary objective of the export-led strategy, it would be a major oversight to ignore the role of the export of labor as part of that strategy.

The Competitive Structure of Labor Markets

While Caribbean exporters seek to widen the market for their exports, Caribbean workers seek to widen the market for their services. We have argued that the growth of wage rates is constrained for the skilled as well as the unskilled. For the unskilled, wage rates are constrained by high unemployment rates, and for the skilled with low unemployment rates, they are constrained by the structure of the labor market. In no other profession is this more apparent than in nursing.

Nurses migrate in large numbers from Jamaica to better paying positions in the United States, creating a shortage in their home country. Despite the shortage, the wage rates have not grown by much. As a result, nurses continue to leave the country. Sometimes an entire graduating class will leave. The central problem is that the domestic market for nurses is not competitive. The government is a virtual monopoly employer. And like all monopoly employers, it tends to pay a wage that is less than the value of the worker's marginal product. By doing so, it is able to thwart the market mechanism and prevent the shortage from pushing wage rates up to a level that would eliminate the shortage. As a result, nurses have redefined their labor market to include the United States.

Nurses have thus made their market more competitive, since foreign employers now compete with the government for their services. Furthermore, with the foreign employers they are more productive, because they work with better equipment on the job. Since they are more productive and since a competitive employer tends to pay a wage that is closer to the worker's marginal product, the nurses receive much higher wages than in their home country, despite the shortage of nurses there. Some nurses move in and out of both markets during the course of a year. Having worked in the United States for six months, they will return to Jamaica for the other six months with the certainty that they will get a job because of the shortage of nurses. Thus the shortage of nurses in Jamaica creates a circulating migratory pattern for some nurses.

Openness, Migration, and Trade

Caribbean countries are often described as open economies. And openness is usually measured as the ratio of foreign trade to the gross domestic product. For some Caribbean countries, the value of foreign trade may exceed their gross domestic product. But openness so measured does not capture the foreign exchange earnings of exported labor. Neither does it capture the fact that some migrants see the labor market in their home country as part of a much larger competitive labor market that includes the United States.

In this larger competitive labor market, the migrant takes his or her services abroad to sell. The worker who produces tradable goods in the sending country embodies his or her labor in the product produced and sells the product abroad. The worker may also produce a good or service that is not tradable—that is, not sold internationally. But whether the worker produces a tradable or nontradable good or service, that worker may decide to sell the service directly abroad by migrating. If the migrant comes from a sector that produces tradable goods, then his or her migration represents a substitute for international trade. The cost of such migration would be more accurately reflected in the export earnings foregone as a result of declining exports. If the migrant comes from the non-tradable sector, then no foreign exchange would be lost.

We are mindful, however, that the productivity of the tradable sector is affected in many ways by the nontradable sector. The delivery of electric power, for example, is important for the assembly of garments. But firms that produce for export often provide their own electric power, especially in countries where central power generation is unreliable. If there are then some cases in which the migration of workers from the nontradable sector does not affect the performance of the tradable sector, it is reasonable to conclude that the impact of such migration on export earnings would be different from that of migration from the tradable sector. While migration data are not broken down in this manner, there are certain occupations that can be easily identified with one sector or another. Given the importance of export earnings in these small open economies, the migration of skilled workers from the tradable sector would tend to impose a greater burden on the sending country than migration of skilled workers from the nontradable sector.

A simple model can illustrate this. Assume a full-employment economy with two sectors, one tradable and one nontradable, each employing 100 workers, and assume wage rates are equal in both sectors. Assume also that there is no movement of workers between the sectors and no impact of nontradable pro-duction on production in the tradable sector. Export earnings of the tradable sector are $500, which is equal to the combined imports of both sectors, each sector importing $250. Now assume that 10 workers migrate from the tradable sector, reducing export earnings by $50 and imports by $25, creating a balance of trade deficit, since imports ($475) would now be greater than exports ($450). Now assume that 10 workers from the nontradable sector migrate. Total imports would fall to $475 while export earnings would remain unchanged at $500, cre-ating a balance of trade surplus. Under these assumptions, we may conclude that a small open economy would be hurt more when workers migrate from the tradable sector than from the nontradable sector.

But what would happen if we relax our assumption about the nonmove-ment of workers between sectors? When workers from the tradable sector emi-grate, the wage rate of those remaining would tend to rise, inducing workers from the nontradable sector to replace those who emigrated. As nontradable sector workers move, wages in that sector would also rise. The net result is an increase in wage rates in both sectors. This would increase the cost of produc-tion and push up the price of exports. If exporters are unable to pass this increase on to foreign buyers, profits in the tradable sector would decline, mak-ing it more difficult to attract investment. So even with the relaxation of assumption on intersectoral labor movement, migration would still have a neg-ative impact on the tradable sector. If we relax the assumption about the impact of nontradable production (banking, insurance, health care, education, etc.) on the tradable sector, migration from some parts of the nontradable sector may have a negative impact on exports. But the impact may not be immediate, as compared with the impact of the migration of workers from the tradable sector.

In this illustration we have assumed full employment. This is not far fetched as it might seem. While high rates of unemployment are typical of Caribbean countries, full employment is not unusual in certain skilled occupations. This illustration brings our trade-migration argument full circle. While trade may affect migration through the creation of employment, migration may affect trade, especially if the migrants are skilled and come from the tradable sector.

A Countermigration of Skilled Workers

While our emphasis so far has been on the outflow of workers, there is a small counterflow. The inflow of foreign investment into Caribbean industries often brings with it a small number of skilled foreign workers to administer the enterprise. In some instances, the inflow of professional foreign workers is induced by vacancies created by emigration. These incoming professionals are typically hired on limited-period contracts at salaries often subsidized by international institutions or foreign governments.

In 1984 the prime minister of Jamaica, Edward Seaga, proposed the creation of an international manpower bank that would supply the kinds of highly skilled people the Caribbean needs. This bank would be administered by an international agency, which would subsidize the salaries of those recruited from abroad (Hope 1985, 254). But an international bank for manpower can be regarded as only a short-term solution. If the skilled foreign workers from such a bank could contribute in concrete ways to the expansion of trade and employment, they would be a valuable resource. It would seem, however, that the creation of a Caribbean *expatriate* manpower bank would probably be more effective in accomplishing this goal because of the built-in desire of many expatriate professionals to contribute not only their skills but their capital to the development of their home countries. Because of the large stock of Caribbean peoples overseas, such a bank would contain a rich diversity of skilled and professional people. It would allow the Caribbean to draw on these expatriate resources in a way that it currently cannot. Because the services of the expatriates would be available at salaries at least equivalent to what they currently receive in the countries in which they reside, Caribbean governments would require international financial support to draw on the resources of the bank. The governments of the major immigrant receiving countries could be called on to fund the bank as part of their development assistance to the Caribbean.

eight

Patterns of the Past and Flows of the Future

The slave trade brought Africans to the Caribbean to work in the sugar cane fields. When slavery was abolished, the colonial planters imported indentured servants from India and China to replace the freed slaves on the plantation. While the availability of cheap labor was the lifeblood of the sugar economies, it stifled any incentive on the part of the planters to modernize their investment by adapting new technology. As a consequence, emancipation and the demise of mercantilism in the latter half of the nineteenth century left the Caribbean sugar economies unprepared to compete with the rest of the world. They were, therefore, unable to provide their populations with an adequate livelihood. It took foreign investment elsewhere in the region to absorb the surplus of unskilled workers. Thus, from emancipation to political independence, which began in the early 1960s, migration from the Caribbean had overwhelmingly been to countries where there was a demand for low-skilled workers.

Up to World War II, Caribbean migration was temporary in character and was primarily a migration of workers as individuals. Since World War II, migration has become overwhelmingly a movement not just of individual workers but of families for settlement in the United Kingdom, Canada, and the United States. Since 1962, when political independence came to the British Caribbean, migration has been primarily to the United States, whose immigration policy has encouraged family unification. This policy recognizes the divisive nature of migration and the importance of a united family in the fabric of American society. This emphasis on family unification stands in sharp contrast to the forced migration under slavery that tore families apart. In the discussion that follows, the household is treated as synonymous with the family and the emphasis is on the household with multiple members. It is recognized that in some households there may be only one person, however, in which case family reunification may not be important.

As discussed in chapter 7, the immigrant household seldom moves as a complete unit. The pattern has been for one adult member to migrate first. Upon employment, the immigrant remits funds to help finance the day-to-day living of those remaining behind as well as their reunification with the new immigrant household abroad. Thus the initial movement to the destination country, followed by a flow of remittances to the country of origin, which helps to finance

77

the movement of the rest of the household to the destination country, might be described as circular, with remittances providing the unifying link.

As long as some members of the household remain behind, remittances will continue to flow. When the household is completely reunited abroad, this flow will cease, or at least diminish, as the circle of migration is closed. The flow of remittances, then, indicates the existence of incomplete migration circles. Because remittances bring with them the powerful message that things are better abroad, they tend to predispose recipients to migrate—even those recipients who are not immediate members of the migrating household.

The mobility of a household depends to a large extent on its composition. A study of family migration decisions in the United States by Jacob Mincer has some relevance for international migration in general and for Caribbean migration in particular. "Married persons are less likely to move than singles," Mincer observes, "and the mobility of separated and divorced partners is by far the highest. The mobility of singles is dampened by the fact that many of them are tied to . . . parents or other close relatives" (Mincer 1978, 771). Mincer points out that "since gains and losses from migration are mainly attributable to job mobility, two earner families are more likely to be deterred than single earner families. Single earners in husband-wife families are almost always men, so it is families with working wives whose migration is most likely to be inhibited" (Mincer 1978, 770). It is reasonable to infer, therefore, that the most mobile households are those headed by single, separated, or divorced persons and those with one-earner, married-couple families. The migration of single, separated, or divorced persons from the Caribbean fits into the circular migration process when the migrants leave their children behind and send for them later. The same is true for the married-couple family when the wife and children subsequently join their husband and father abroad.

There is a high share of women among Caribbean immigrants. And there is a high probability that most of the women who leave their children behind are single parents. This is based on the fact that the share of children born out of wedlock is extremely high. In Jamaica, for example, from which the largest share of English-speaking Caribbean immigrants come, this share exceeded 75 percent between 1967 and 1977 (Department of Statistics, Jamaica 1979, 20, 29). The mobility of these women with children is facilitated by the extended family, typically an aunt or a maternal grandparent who often takes care of the children until they are sent for.

Although in a married-couple family the decision to migrate is usually made by the husband, it is sometimes made by the wife, for whom there are usually better opportunities for employment abroad. In this case, the reunification of the household abroad will depend on the perceived ease with which the husband may find a comparable job. Aubrey Bonnett observes that in some instances, the reunification does not work because the new economic and social independence achieved by the wife clashes with the traditional expectation of the husband (Bonnett 1990, 115–38). Given the fact that in Caribbean households there is a disproportionate share of single parents and common-law arrangements and that the one earner married couple is still the norm, it is reasonable to conclude that these households have an unusual degree of mobility and that this mobility is reflected in the high propensity to migrate from the region.

The movement begins when a member of the household makes the decision to enhance the lifetime income of the household by seeking employment abroad. This decision is based on the knowledge of employment opportunities abroad gathered from relatives and friends who have migrated, from published sources, or from potential employers. The decision is usually motivated by the wide disparity between earnings at home and earnings abroad as well as by the limited employment choices at home. The limited employment choices and the lower level of earnings are themselves determined by the structure of the home economy, which is itself shaped by the history of sugar and the small size of the countries.

The quality of labor is also influenced by the structure of the economy. Because the Caribbean has come late to industrial development, its labor force has not accumulated those skills required by complex industrial processes. As a producer of goods requiring relatively simple technology, the productivity of workers in the region has been relatively low, except in those few industries that are capital intensive. This low labor productivity is aggravated by the high rate of underemployment. As a consequence, wage rates are low relative to those in industrial countries where workers are generally more productive because they work with more and better capital equipment. Against this background, the Caribbean worker with transferable skills makes the decision to migrate.

The Demand for Labor in the United States

Immigrants have historically filled jobs at the bottom of the employment structure in America. Today, as American industry moves into areas of higher technology, large numbers of jobs, many of them paying a low wage, are being created in the service sector. In its *Workforce 2000*, the Hudson Institute points out that the country's demand for low-skilled workers will continue to be substantial: "Although the overall pattern of job growth is weighted toward higher skilled occupations, very large numbers of jobs will be created in some medium- to low-skilled fields. In absolute numbers, the biggest job creation categories will be in service occupations, administrative support, and marketing and sales, which together account for half of the net new jobs that will be created. In the service category, the largest groups are cooks, nursing aides, waiters, and janitors. Among administrative support jobs, secretaries, clerks, and computer operators predominate. In marketing and sales, most of the new slots will be for cashiers. With the exception of computer operators, most of these large categories require only modest levels of skill" (Hudson Institute 1987, 99).

The majority of the Caribbean immigrants in the United States work in this rapidly expanding service sector. Because the greatest concentration of these immigrants can be found in the State of New York and because many of them are employed in health and private household services, it is instructive to examine the future trend of employment in these occupations in that state. The Bureau of Economic Analysis of the U.S. Department of Commerce projects that between 1988 and 2040, employment and average earnings (in 1982 dollars) in health services in New York will increase by 15.2 percent and 64.6 percent, respectively. The employment of private household workers, however, will decline by 27.8 percent. The data in table 8.1 indicate that as the service sector grows, the fastest growth in employment will occur in business, health, and

Table 8.1

Projected Growth of Income and Employment in Selected Services
New York State, 1988–2040

Type of Service	Total Earnings (Mill. 1982 U.S.$)		Employment (000)		Average Earnings	
	1988	2040	1988	2040	1988	2040
All Services	60,075	113,724	3,027	3,506	19,848	32,439
Private household	740	813	119	86	6,192	9,428
Business	14,465	24,417	722	977	20,042	24,992
Health	15,459	29,304	696	802	22,201	36,548
Legal	7,366	15,889	149	181	49,472	87,735
Educational	3,642	6,146	257	274	14,182	22,413
Misc. prof.	6,868	12,224	197	213	34,863	57,388

Source: U.S. Department of Commerce, Bureau of Economic Analysis, *BEA Regional Projections to 2040* (Washington, D.C.: U.S. Government Printing Office, 1990).

legal services and that business and health services will continue to account for roughly half the employment in services. So, even if the demand for Caribbean women for private household work dries up, there will continue to be a strong demand for Caribbean workers in health services.

The Immigration and Nationality Act of 1990, which became effective in 1992, has increased the annual number of visas to be issued for those with needed professional skills from 54,000 to 140,000 and has reduced the number available for low-skilled immigrants from 18,000 to 10,000. Some employers believe the reduction in the number of visas for low-skilled immigrants will lead to a shortage of private household workers, creating a "nanny problem" (Vobejda 1990, A4). Employers in other labor-intensive industries, such as hotels, restaurants, and poultry processing, are also reported to worry about the potential shortage of low-skilled labor (Vobejda 1990, A4).

The reduction of available visas legislated by the Immigration and Nationality Act does not necessarily mean that the flow of low-skilled workers will decline. Of the overall annual limit of 700,000 immigrant visas set by the 1990 law, up to 480,000 will be made available to the families of U.S. citizens and permanent residents. This means that the United States will continue to receive large inflows of immigrants from countries that have been major sources of immigrants since 1965 as families are reunited; and since a large share of these family members will be spouses and dependents who generally have low skills, the flow of low-skilled immigrants will continue through the family-unification provisions of the law.

Chiswick argues that more than half of the 54,000 visas that were available annually for professional and other skilled workers prior to the 1990 law went to spouses and dependent children of applicants who were "generally lesser-skilled individuals." Chiswick also points out that "the sixth preference for 'skilled workers and other workers in labor shortage' is a vehicle for the entry of cooks, baby sitters and other low skilled workers. About half of the recipients of sixth preference visas in 1989 (excluding spouses and children) were non-professional service occupations" (Chiswick 1990, D3). The point of all this is that a disproportionate share of low-skilled immigrants enter the United States under the preference for skilled workers.

Success for the children of the new immigrants who arrive with low skills will depend increasingly on the amount of investment in their education. As the Hudson Institute puts it, "During the 1985–2000 period, the good fortune to be born in or to immigrate to the United States will make less difference than the luck or the initiative to be well-educated and well-trained" (Hudson Institute 1987, 103). This assessment is supported by the *Economist* in its weekly American survey: "The premium in higher earnings that rewards better education and greater skills has never been bigger" (*Economist* 1990, 22).

Return Migration

Historically, return migration has been an important feature of Caribbean migration. In the days when migration was a temporary movement of people in search of work, large return flows were a predictable part of the pattern. Today, the return flows are less predictable and more difficult to measure. The overwhelming character of migration today is a movement of families for settlement abroad. These migrants become permanent residents and many of them citizens.

While the achievement of permanent-resident status and citizenship in the United States typically indicates that the migrant is here to settle, it does not rule out a return to the country of origin after retirement. Neither does it rule out a return before retirement. Indeed, it may be argued that the acquisition of permanent residency status or citizenship widens the job options of the immigrant as long as he or she does not have to give up citizenship in the country of origin. The immigrant can choose to return to work in the country of origin if he or she later deems the opportunities there to be more attractive than those in the United States.

Although the figures are not available, it is well known that in Jamaica a large number of professionals in top positions in government and business who have lived for some time in the United States still hold onto their resident alien identification cards, popularly known as "green cards". Among this group are some high-ranking politicians. The green card makes travel between the United States and the Caribbean easy, and it offers an out for those whose future job security at home is less than certain.

Elizabeth Thomas-Hope breaks down long-term migrants who have returned home into three categories: settlers, students and other young persons, and long-term circulators. Settlers who return after 20 or 30 years abroad have the greatest problem readjusting to the social and economic environment of their country of birth. Those who return with some capital typically start small retail businesses in the localities where they were born. Surveys have shown that no more than 5 percent of them return after retirement, and they tend to be "those whose occupations overseas were related to the labor demands of industrialized countries, and they thus acquired few if any skills relevant to the work opportunities in their homeland" (Thomas-Hope 1985, 160).

Yet many long-term migrants who have studied and worked abroad do return with valuable and relevant skills. After completing their university degrees, many of them acquire permanent residency status and even citizenship in the United States. Although no data are available on the return flow of these migrants, anecdotal evidence indicates that many highly trained professionals have returned to take top positions in Jamaica and elsewhere in the Caribbean since political independence began in the 1960s. Some who returned did not stay because they were unable to adjust to certain local social attitudes that they regarded as provincial. Of those who stayed, many have made significant contributions to their country of birth in government and business.

Thomas-Hope describes the long-term circulators as "those individuals who repeatedly go overseas, usually to the same country, reentering the job market each time and becoming a permanent resident of that country or even a citizen" (Thomas-Hope 1985, 162). They generally regard the Caribbean as home and the foreign country as the workplace, and they tend to be domestic servants or nurses. Since they regard the Caribbean as home, they remit a large share of their modest income back to the home country, primarily for building a house.

The pursuit of free-market development strategies by the English-speaking Caribbean countries offers the prospect of new opportunities in the private sector for highly trained immigrants who wish to return. This, coupled with the emergence of a conscious policy on the part of some Caribbean governments to utilize the vast stock of Caribbean human capital abroad on a temporary as well as on a permanent basis, may stimulate the return flow of more expatriate professionals. In 1993 the government of Jamaica, in cooperation with the Commission of the European Communities and the International Organization for Migration (IOM), embarked on a program called Migration for Development. The intent of the program is to facilitate the return and reintegration, over a two and a half-year period, of 40 professional Jamaican nationals residing in industrialized countries "to fill important vacant development positions" such as managers, engineers, and policy analysts. (International Organization for Migration 1993, 2).

The program is administered by the IOM, which is composed of 52 member states and 41 observer states. Established in Brussels in 1951, the IOM has as its mission, among other things, the handling of "the orderly and planned migration of nationals to meet the specific needs of sending and receiving countries; [and] the transfer of qualified human resources to promote the economic, social and cultural advancement of developing countries" (International Organization for Migration 1993, 6).

Migration for Development provides the following incentives to those who wish to return: travel expenses for the returnee and his or her family; a fixed amount for the transport of luggage and personal effects; reintegration support to supplement housing and living costs for a fixed period; medical and accident insurance for the returnee and his or her family for a fixed period; topping up of salary for a fixed period; and support for the acquisition of scientific and/or professional equipment and/or literature necessary to perform the job.

Migration as a Part of a Larger Population Movement

The political scientist and Caribbeanist Gordon K. Lewis observes that "the essence of Caribbean life has always been movement. It explains the energizing brio of Caribbean life in music and dance, sports, language, even religion and politics. It also explains, of course, the socio-economic phenomenon of migration" (Lewis 1990, xiii). Migration, however, is only part of the population movement out of and into the Caribbean. Millions of tourists travel to the region each year, mostly from North America, and thousands of Caribbean people move in the other direction as temporary visitors. The immigrants move to improve their economic condition. The North American tourist is a reflection of the better economic conditions in North America to which the immigrants aspire. And tourists from the Caribbean are a reflection of their relative affluence in their respective countries.

The tourist/immigrant composition of the population movement from the Caribbean is determined by such factors as the level of Caribbean development relative to that of the United States, proximity to the United States, and the behavior of currency exchange rates. Table 8.2 depicts the ratio of immigrants to temporary visitors from Jamaica, the Dominican Republic, Haiti, Barbados, and Trinidad and Tobago for the years 1966–75, a period in which exchange rates were relatively stable. Given stable exchange rates, differences in the immigrant/temporary visitors ratio would have to be attributed to differences in per capita income and the cost of transportation.

The Dominican Republic, only a few miles west of Puerto Rico, a U.S. territory, is closest to the United States. Trinidad and Barbados are the farthest away. If we weight the cost of transportation from the Dominican Republic to Puerto Rico with an index of 100, the index for each of the other countries would exceed 100. Since greater distance does not mean proportionally greater transportation cost, we assign the following weights for transportation cost: Haiti

Table 8.2

Ratio of Immigrants (I) to Temporary Visitors (TV) from the Caribbean, 1966–1975

Country	TV	I	I:TV	Weights	Weighted I:TV
Barbados	59,432	15,190	1:3.9	300	1:11.7
Dom. Rep.	537,418	125,795	1:4.2	100	1:4.2
Haiti	128,965	54,778	1:2.3	150	1:3.4
Jamaica	409,302	124,121	1:3.2	200	1:6.4
Trinidad and Tobago	195,541	55,645	1:3.5	300	1:10.5

Source: Immigration and Naturalization Service, Annual Report 1975 (Washington, D.C., 1975).

150, Jamaica 200, and Barbados and Trinidad 300. To eliminate the impact of transportation cost on the ratio of immigrants to temporary visitors, we multiply the number of temporary visitors per immigrant for each country by its respective weight. The results in table 8.2 show Haiti with the lowest number of temporary visitors per immigrant and Barbados with the highest. This conforms quite closely to the per capita distribution of income among the countries. In its income classification of developing countries, the World Bank ranks Barbados and Trinidad as upper middle income, Jamaica and the Dominican Republic as middle income, and Haiti as low income.

As the income gap between the United States and the Caribbean narrows, the share of Caribbean tourists in the outward population movement is likely to increase. But the evolution of the migration process will also transform immigrants into tourists. Once the economic condition of Caribbean immigrants abroad improves, they will more than likely join the stream of tourists visiting their home countries. The character of this Caribbean expatriate tourism may be somewhat different from the sun-and-beach tourism of the typical North American tourist, but it is tourism nonetheless.

If immigrants to the United States are ultimately able to return to the Caribbean as tourists as a result of their improved economic condition, and if more people from the Caribbean are able to travel as tourists to the United States as a result of their improved economic condition, then it is reasonable to say that the economic transformation of the Caribbean household at home or abroad leads to a population movement that is largely a movement of tourists. The United States benefits when the transformation takes place there, because the immigrants add to the national wealth. Despite the flow of remittances from the immigrants, the Caribbean benefits more when the transformation takes place in the Caribbean. What determines where the transformation takes place is really the crux of the migration phenomenon.

If we accept the argument that this transformation in the Caribbean will be determined largely by greater domestic investment in export industries and wider access of exports to foreign markets, then we need to look at the tourist industry itself, since it is the major earner of foreign exchange for the region. In Jamaica, for example, tourism far outstrips such traditional exports as alumina, bauxite, and sugar in the generation of foreign exchange earnings. (See table 8.3.) This brings up the question, Can the tourism industry in the Caribbean stimulate the kind of development that will enable potential migrants to improve their economic condition at home? The answer lies in the extent to which tourism can stimulate a diversified economy capable of absorbing the labor force in a wide range of good paying jobs.

Dependence on tourism subjects Caribbean economies to the ebb and flow of the economies from which the tourists come, as well as to unforeseen international events that interrupt the flow of tourists. Yet the benefits from climate and geography make this industry immensely attractive. The owners of hotels and other tourist facilities do not bear the cost of providing the beach and the scenery; they bear only the cost of providing access to them. Part of their total revenues thus represents payment for these gifts of nature, which they did not provide. Economists call this a surplus, or economic rent. The tourist industry can capture this surplus only if there is a demand for Caribbean tourism. If there is no demand, there is no surplus.

Table 8.3

Comparison of Foreign Exchange Earnings of Tourism and Other Leading Exports, 1981–1987 (Millions of U.S.$)

Year	Tourism	Alumina	Bauxite	Sugar
1981	284.3	588.2	172.0	46.5
1982	337.8	354.8	129.6	47.7
1983	399.2	199.2	67.1	34.4
1984	406.6	258.3	119.9	34.8
1985	406.8	211.1	85.9	46.1
1986	516.0	210.7	97.4	43.6
1987	595.0	199.3	113.9	61.5

Sources: World Bank, *Caribbean Countries: Economic Situation, Regional Issues, And Capital Flows* (Washington, D.C., 1988); International Monetary Fund, *International Financial Statistics* (Washington, D.C., 1988).

As a service industry, tourism has another important advantage. It does not depend on economies of scale to the extent that manufacturing industries do. With economies of scale, larger size means greater efficiency. In tourism the small firm can be just as efficient as the large firm. Therefore, there tends to be a wide variety of sizes in tourist enterprises, each one capable of being profitable. This allows for greater local participation in tourism than in manufacturing, where size is important for efficiency. Despite this advantage, the countries of the region actively pursue a strategy of economic diversification and trade expansion to stimulate the growth of employment and income.

Accelerated Growth as the Antidote to Migration

In the 1980s, the centerpiece of U.S. policy toward the Caribbean was the Caribbean Basin Initiative, which provided duty-free access to a range of imports from the Caribbean. This policy was based on the premise that greater access to U.S. markets by Caribbean countries would stimulate the economic development of the region, which would in turn ensure political stability and reduce the propensity of Caribbean people to migrate legally and illegally to the United States. Because Caribbean migration to the United States is driven primarily by economics, this argument is theoretically sound. For this policy to have worked in practice, however, it would have had to do more than create jobs; it would have had to reduce the gap in wages and living standards between the Caribbean and the United States; between 1980 and 1987, this gap widened. Table 8.4 shows that GNP per capita in Haiti, the Dominican Republic, Jamaica, and Trinidad and Tobago declined relative to that of the United States; in

Table 8.4

GNP Per Capita: United States and the Caribbean, 1980 and 1987

Country	1980	Index	1987	Index
Haiti	$270	2.3	$360	1.9
Jamaica	1,040	9.1	940	5.0
Dom. Rep.	1,160	10.2	730	3.9
Trin. and Tob.	4,370	38.5	4,210	22.7
United States	11,360	100.0	18,530	100.0

Sources: World Bank, *World Development Report, 1982* and *1989* (New York: Oxford University Press, 1982, 1989).

Jamaica, the Dominican Republic, and Trinidad and Tobago, the decline was absolute. To reduce this disparity, the rate of economic growth in these countries would have had to outstrip that of the United States by a wide margin. World Bank data show that between 1980 and 1987, Haiti had an average annual growth rate of gross domestic product of –0.4 percent, Jamaica 0.4 percent, the Dominican Republic 1.6 percent, and Trinidad and Tobago –6.1 percent. Over the same period, annual population growth in these countries averaged 1.8 percent, compared with 1.0 percent in the United States. The result of all this has been a general decline in the standard of living in the Caribbean. Even if the absolute decline is reversed, it is harder to reverse the relative decline without a massive infusion of capital into these small economies. This is not likely to take the form of increased aid from the U.S. government because of the constraints placed on spending by its budget deficit problem. It must come from private foreign investment.

Most of the private foreign investment in the Caribbean over the past decade has gone into labor-intensive assembly operations attracted by low-wage labor. While this kind of production generates foreign exchange, its impact on economic development is limited. Moreover, cheap labor is an uncertain foundation for a development strategy because it can easily be undermined by more efficient labor elsewhere. The North American Free Trade Agreement (NAFTA) between the United States, Canada, and Mexico is a potential threat to some of these labor-intensive assembly operations in the Caribbean. The removal of all tariff and nontariff barriers between Mexico and the United States is expected to divert some trade in these labor-intensive products from the Caribbean to Mexico unless Caribbean exports receive similar treatment. It is, therefore, in the interest of those Caribbean countries with significant offshore apparel-assembly production to become a part of NAFTA.

In 1990, the George Bush administration proposed its Enterprise for the Americas Initiative, which would allow each Caribbean and Latin American country to enter a framework agreement with the United States for negotiating an ultimate removal of all trade barriers. Not all countries feel that their economies are strong enough to withstand the onslaught of open competition from U.S. firms. Small Caribbean economies still feel a need to protect their less efficient industries. The fact that they have historically depended on preferential markets has made them unprepared for open competition. They argue, in general, that although the United States is their major export market, their exports to the United States constitute only a small fraction of total U.S. imports; they would therefore like the United States to remove all its trade barriers without being asked to reciprocate. Despite this argument, the United States insists on some reciprocity because it now likens unreasonable barriers to exports as a threat to its own national security. This position is underscored by U.S. trade representative Mickey Kantor: "We will focus our energies on whatever barriers— government or private, visible or hidden—that restrict access of competitive American firms to foreign markets" (Kantor 1993, B1).

Many Caribbean countries are in the process of freeing up their economies by reversing the massive intrusion of government into the private sector over the past two decades. The objective is to increase the growth of the economy by letting market forces operate more efficiently. This is a prerequisite for competing in a world increasingly dominated by large trading blocs. This will not wipe out such migration-inducing factors as the restraint on wages by the monopsonistic structure of domestic labor markets and the demand for Caribbean workers by an expanding U.S. service economy. But the influence of these factors on the decision to migrate is likely to lessen if freer markets accelerate economic growth in the region.

Notes

three

1. Roy Bryce-Laporte provides an abbreviated list of other "outstanding personalities among those with West Indian birth and ancestry who have helped shape American history—Crispus Attucks, Alexander Hamilton, Edward Blyden, Marcus Garvey, John B. Russwurm, Bert Williams, Prince Hall, Jan Matzeliger, Hugh Mulgaz, Samuel Wood, Claude McKay, and Arthur Schomberg. A younger generation consists of Kenneth B. Clark, Oliver Cromwell Cox, Hazel Scott, Harry Belafonte, Sidney Poitier, Stokely Carmichael, Pearl Primus, Geoffrey Holder, Rod Carew, Elliott Skinner, . . . Monty Alexander, Mongo Santamaria, and Patrick Ewing. Among those of second or subsequent generation West Indian Americans are Shirley Chisholm, Clifford Alexander, Cicely Tyson, Paule Marshall, June Jordan, Kareem Abdul-Jabbar, Marcus Alexis, St. Clair Drake, Constance Mottley, Barbara Jackson, Vincent Harding, Leroi Jones, and Franklyn Thomas" (Bryce-Laporte 1983, 2).

According to Miriam Klevan, the Jamaican John B. Russwurm listed above was the first black person to graduate from an American college and the first to publish a newspaper in the United States (Klevan 1990, 15). Klevan also notes that black American author James Weldon Johnson is of West Indian ancestry. His mother was from the Bahamas (Klevan 1990, 67–70). To this list must be added the name of the Muslim activist Malcolm X (born Malcolm Little), whose mother was from Grenada and whose father was a white American.

There are some notable British West Indian immigrants who came to America in the eighteenth century; two, Alexander Hamilton and Alexander James Dallas, deserve special mention.

Alexander Hamilton was born in 1755 on the island of Nevis, the illegitimate son of James Hamilton, a Scotsman, and Rachel Fawcett Lavien, daughter of a doctor-planter on Nevis and the estranged wife of a merchant. Alexander went to the North American colonies in 1772 and studied at Kings College (now Columbia) in 1773–74. He wrote numerous papers and pamphlets in support of the American Revolution and later became George Washington's secretary and aide-de-camp. His impressive contributions to the Federalist Papers played a major role in getting the Constitution ratified. He became the first secretary of the Treasury under George Washington.

Alexander James Dallas was born in Jamaica in 1759; he was U.S. secretary of the State Department from 1791 to 1801 and secretary of the Treasury from

1814 to 1816. His son, George Mifflin Dallas, after whom the city of Dallas, Texas, is named, was vice president of the United States from 1845 to 1849.

four

1. There are some exceptions to this general rule. Satellite technology has allowed airline companies to transfer ticket-processing work to offshore locations where wage rates are considerably lower. And at least one major hotel chain has transferred its reservation service offshore.

2. The Immigration Act of 1965, which became effective in 1968, imposed a numerical ceiling of 170,000 on immigration from the Eastern Hemisphere and 120,000 on immigration from the Western Hemisphere. Immigration from the Eastern Hemisphere was apportioned on the basis of a system of seven preference categories. In 1977, these categories were adapted to immigration from the West. In 1978, the hemisphere limits were abolished and replaced by a worldwide limit of 290,000. And in 1980, the seventh preference category for refugees was removed from this worldwide limit. The following is a description of the remaining six preference categories along with the percentage of all immigrants admitted under the numerical ceiling: first, unmarried adult sons of U.S. citizens (20 percent); second, spouses and unmarried adult sons and daughters of aliens lawfully admitted for permanent residence (26 percent); third, members of professions or persons of exceptional ability in the arts and sciences (10 percent); fourth, married sons and daughters of U.S. citizens, 21 years of age and over (24 percent); sixth, skilled and unskilled workers in occupations for which labor is in short supply (10 percent). Numbers not used by these preferences are made available to qualified nonpreference immigrants. Immediate relatives of U.S. citizens and various classes of special immigrants are exempt from the numerical ceiling.

References

Ayearst, Morley. 1960. *The British West Indies: The Search for Self-Government.* New York: New York University Press.

Basch, Linda. 1987. "The Politics of Caribbeanization: Vincentians and Grenadians in New York." In *Caribbean Life in New York City: Sociological Dimensions,* edited by Constance R. Sutton and Elsa M. Chaney. New York: Center for Migration Studies.

Beachey, R. W. 1957. *The British West Indies Sugar Industry in the Late Nineteenth Century.* Oxford: Basil Blackwell.

Bernard, William S. 1982. "A History of U.S. Immigration Policy." In *Immigration: Dimensions of Ethnicity,* edited by Richard A. Easterlin et al. Cambridge, Mass.: Harvard University Press.

Berry, R. Albert, and Ronald Soligo. 1969. "Some Welfare Aspects of International Migration." *Journal of Political Economy* 77.

Bhagwati, J. N., and M. Partington, eds. 1976. *Taxing the Brain Drain: A Proposal.* New York: North-Holland Publishing Co.

Bogen, Elizabeth. 1987. *Immigration in New York.* New York: Praeger.

Bonnett, Aubrey W. 1981. *Institutional Adaptation of West Indian Immigrants to America: An Analysis of Rotating Credit Associations.* Washington, D.C., University Press of America.

———. 1990. "The New Female West Indian Immigrant: Dilemmas of Coping in the Host Society." In *In Search of a Better Life: Perspectives on Migration from the Caribbean,* edited by Ransford W. Palmer. New York: Praeger.

Briggs, Vernon M. 1992. *Mass Immigration and the National Interest.* Armonk, N.Y.: M. E. Sharpe.

Bryce-Laporte, Roy Simon. 1972. "Black Immigrants: The Experience of Inequality and Invisibility." *Journal of Black Studies,* 3.

———. 1983. "West Indian Immigrants: Their Presence, Experiences, and Contributions." *Urban Review* 9.

Caplovitz, David. 1973. *The Merchants of Harlem: A Study of Small Business in a Black Community.* Beverly Hills, Calif.: Sage Publications.

Chevannes, Barry, and Heather Ricketts. 1993. "Return Migration and Small Business Development in Jamaica." Unpublished paper, University of the West Indies, Mona, Jamaica.

Chisholm, Shirley. 1970. *Shirley Chislom: Unbought and Unbossed.* New York: Avon Books.

Chiswick, Barry R. 1980. "Immigrant Earnings Pattern by Sex, Race, and Ethnic Groupings." *Monthly Labor Review* 103.

———. 1990. "Opening the Golden Door." *Washington Post*, 7 October.

Department of Statistics. 1979. *Demographic Statistics*. Kingston, Jamaica: Government Printer.

Economic and Social Survey Jamaica 1979. 1980. Kingston, Jamaica: Government Printing Office.

Economist. "American Survey," 10 November 1990.

Eisner, Gisela. 1961. *Jamaica, 1830–1930: A Study in Economic Growth*. Manchester, England: Manchester University Press.

Foner, Nancy. 1987. "West Indians in New York City and London: A Comparative Analysis." In *Caribbean Life in New York City: Sociocultural Dimensions*, edited by Constance R. Sutton and Elsa M. Chaney. New York: Center for Migration Studies of New York.

Forsythe, Dennis. 1976. "Black Immigrants and the American Ethos: Theories and Observations." In *Caribbean Immigration to the United States*, edited by Roy Bryce-Laporte and Delores Mortimer. Washington, D.C.: Research Institute on Immigration and Ethnic Studies, Smithsonian Institution.

Frank, Harry A. 1920. *Roaming through the West Indies*. New York: Blue Ribbon Books.

Fraser, Peter. 1990. "Nineteenth-Century West Indian Migration to Britain." In *In Search of a Better Life: Perspectives on Migration from the Caribbean*, edited by Ransford W. Palmer. New York: Praeger.

Freeman, Gary P. "Caribbean Migration to Britain and France: From Assimilation to Selection." 1990. In *The Caribbean Exodus*, edited by Barry B. Levine. New York: Praeger.

Glazer, Nathan, and Daniel Patrick Moynihan. 1963. *Beyond the Melting Pot: The Negroes, Puerto Ricans, Jews, Italians, and Irish of New York City*. Cambridge: MIT Press.

Gordon, Monica H. 1990. "Dependents or Workers?: The Status of Caribbean Immigrant Women in the United States." In *In Search of a Better Life: Perspectives on Migration from the Caribbean*, edited by Ransford W. Palmer. New York: Praeger.

Green, Charles, and Basil Wilson. 1989. *The Struggle for Black Empowerment in New York City: Beyond the Politics of Pigmentation*. New York: Praeger.

Griffith, David. 1986. "Peasants in Reserve: Temporary West Indian Labor in the U.S. Farm Labor Market." *International Migration Review* 20.

Grunwald, Henry. 1985. "Home Is Where You Are Happy." *Time*, 8 July.

Gugliotta, Guy. 1990. "Sweetening U.S. Sugar Prices: An Ingrained Program." *Washington Post*, 16 July.

Guyana Development Programme, 1966–1972. 1966. Georgetown, Guyana: Government Printery.

Handlin, Oscar. 1959. *The Newcomers: Negroes and Puerto Ricans in a Changing Metropole*. Cambridge: Harvard University Press.

Holder, Calvin B. 1987. "The Causes and Composition of West Indian Immigration to New York City, 1900–1952." *Afro-Americans in New York Life and History*, January.

Hope, Trevor J. 1985. "The Impact of Immigration on Caribbean Development." In *Migration and Development in the Caribbean: The Unexplored Connection*, edited by Robert A. Pastor. Boulder, Colo.: Westview Press.

Hudson Institute. 1987. *Workforce 2000: Work and Workers for the Twenty-First Century.* Indianapolis.

International Organization of Migration. 1993. *Return and Reintegration Programme of Qualified Jamaican Nationals for Development.* Washington, D.C.

Justus, Joyce Bennett. 1976. "West Indians in Los Angeles: Community and Identity." In *Caribbean Immigration to the United States,* edited by Roy S. Bryce-Laporte and Delores M. Mortimer. Washington, D.C.: Research Institute on Immigration and Ethnic Studies, Smithsonian Institution.

Kantor, Mickey. 1993. "Trade Policies and NAFTA Nerves." *Washington Times,* 21 March.

Kaplan, Irving, et al., eds. 1976. *Area Handbook for Jamaica.* Washington, D.C.: U.S. Government Printing Office.

Kasinitz, Philip. 1988. "From Ghetto Elite to Service Sector: A Comparison of Two Waves of West Indian Immigrants in New York City." *Ethnic Groups* 7.

Klevan, Miriam. 1990. *The West Indian Americans.* New York: Chelsea House Publishers.

Kolack, Shirley. 1980. "Lowell, An Immigrant City: The Old and the New." In *Sourcebook on the New Immigration: Implications for the United States and the International Community,* edited by Roy Bryce-Laporte. New Brunswick, N.J.: Transaction Books.

Lewis, Gordon K. Foreword. 1968. *The Growth of the Modern West Indies.* New York: Monthly Review Press.

————. 1990. In *In Search of a Better Life: Perspectives on Migration from the Caribbean,* edited by Ransford W. Palmer. New York: Praeger.

McCoy, Terry L., and Charles H. Wood. 1982. *Caribbean Workers in the Florida Sugar Industry.* Paper no. 2. Gainesville: Center for Latin American Studies, University of Florida.

Marshall, Dawn. 1985. "Migration and Development in the Eastern Caribbean." In *Migration and Development in the Caribbean: The Unexplored Connection,* edited by Robert A. Pastor. Boulder, Colo.: Westview Press.

————. 1987. "A History of West Indian Migration: Overseas Opportunities and 'Safety-Valve' Policies." In *The Caribbean Exodus,* edited by Barry B. Levine. New York: Praeger.

Miller, Harris. 1985. "U.S. Immigration Policy and Caribbean Economic Development." In *Migration and Development in the Caribbean: The Unexplored Connection,* edited by Robert A. Pastor. Boulder, Colo.: Westview Press.

Mincer, Jacob. 1978. "Family Migration Decisions." *Journal of Political Economy* 86 (October).

Mordecai, John. 1968. *The West Indies: The Federal Negotiations.* London: George Allen and Unwin.

Morris, Margaret. 1979. "What's Air Jamaica's Future?" *Jamaican Weekly Gleaner* (NA), 24 December.

Palmer, Ransford W. 1968. *The Jamaican Economuy.* New York: Praeger.

————. 1979. *Caribbean Dependence on the United States Economy.* New York: Praeger.

————. 1990. "Illegal Migration from the Caribbean." In *In Search of a Better Life: Perspectives on Migration from the Caribbean,* edited by Ransford W. Palmer. New York: Praeger.

————. 1990. *In Search of a Better Life: Perspectives on Migration from the Caribbean.* New York: Praeger.

Pastor, Robert A. 1985. "Introduction: The Policy Challenge." In *Migration and Development in the Caribbean: The Unexplored Connection*, edited by Robert A. Pastor. Boulder, Colo.: Westview Press.

—————. 1987. "The Impact of U.S. Immigration Policy on Caribbean Emigration: Does It Matter?" In *The Caribbean Exodus*, edited by Barry B. Levine. New York: Praeger.

—————, and Rosemarie Rogers. 1985. Using Migration to Enhance Economic Development in the Caribbean: Three Sets of Proposals." In *Migration and Development in the Caribbean: The Unexplored Connection*, edited by Robert A. Pastor. Boulder, Colo.: Westview Press.

Petras, Elizabeth M. 1981. "The Global Labor Market in the Modern World Economy." In *Global Trends in Migration: Theory and Research on International Population Movements*, edited by Mary M. Kritz, Charles B. Keely, and Silvano M. Tomasi. New York: Center for Migration Studies.

Pido, Anthony A. J. 1980. "New Structures, New Immigrants: The Case of the Pilipinos." In *Sourcebook on the New Immigration: Implications for the United States and the International Community*, edited by Roy Bryce-Laporte. New Brunswick, N.J.: Transaction Books.

Portes, Alejandro, and Alex Stepick. 1985. "Unwelcome Immigrants: The Labor Market Experiences of 1980 (Mariel) Cuban and Haitian Refugees in South Florida." *American Sociological Review* 50.

Power, Jonathan. 1979. *Migrant Workers in Western Europe and the United States.* Oxford: Pergamon Press.

Richardson, Bonham C. 1983. *Caribbean Migrants: Environment and Human Survival in St. Kitts and Nevis.* Knoxville: University of Tennessee Press.

—————. 1985. *Panama Money in Barbados, 1900–1920.* Knoxville: University of Tennessee Press.

Richardson, Lisa. 1989. "City's West Indians Put Politics in Spotlight." *Hartford Courant*, metro final ed., 2 August.

Roberts, George W. 1962. "Prospects for Population Growth in the West Indies." *Social and Economic Studies* 11.

Rubenstein, Hyme. 1982. "The Impact of Remittances in Rural English-Speaking Caribbean: Notes on the Literature." In *Migration and Remittances: Developing a Caribbean Perspective*, edited by William F. Stinner, Klaus de Albuquerque, and Roy S. Bryce-Laporte. Washington, D.C.: Research Institute on Immigration and Ethnic Studies, Smithsonian Institution.

Runcie, John. 1986. "Marcus Garvey and the Harlem Renaissance." *Afro-Americans in New York Life and History*, July.

Simon, Julian L. 1989. *The Economic Consequences of Immigration.* Oxford: Basil Blackwell.

Smith, T. E. 1981. *Commonwealth Migration: Flows and Policies.* London: Macmillan Press.

Sowell, Thomas. 1975. *Race and Economics.* New York: David McKay Co.

Sutton, Constance R. 1987. "The Caribbeanization of New York City and the Emergence of a Transnational Socio-Cultural System." In *Caribbean Life in New York City: Sociocultural Dimensions*, edited by Constance R. Sutton and Elsa M. Chaney. New York: Center for Migration Studies of New York.

Thomas, Bert J. 1988. "Historical Functions of Caribbean-American Benevolent/Progressive Associations." *Afro-Americans in New York Life and History*, July.

Thomas-Hope, Elizabeth M. 1985. "Return Migration and Its Implications for Caribbean Development." In *Migration and Development in the Caribbean: The Unexplored Connection,* edited by Robert A. Pastor. Boulder, Colo.: Westview Press.

Thompson, Mel E. 1990. "Forty-and-One Years On: An Overview of Afro-Caribbean Migration to the United Kingdom." In *In Search of a Better Life: Perspectives on Migration from the Caribbean,* edited by Ransford W. Palmer. New York: Praeger.

Traub, James. "You Can Get It If You Really Want." *Harper's,* June 1982.

U.S. Bureau of the Census. 1983. *Census of Population 1980: General Social and Economic Characteristics, New York.* Washington, D.C.: U.S. Government Printing Office.

———. *County Business Patterns, Florida: 1972, 1987.* 1974, 1989. Washington, D.C.: U.S. Government Printing Office.

———. *County Business Patterns, New York: 1972, 1987.* 1974, 1989. Washington, D.C.: U.S. Government Printing Office.

U.S. Department of Commerce, Bureau of the Census. 1988. *Statistical Yearbook of the United States, 1988.* Washington, D.C.: U.S. Government Printing Office.

U.S. Department of Labor, Bureau of International Affairs. 1989. "The Effect of Immigration on the U.S. Economy and Labor Market." In *The President's Comprehensive Triennial Report on Immigration, 1989.* Washington, D.C.: U.S. Government Printing Office.

U.S. International Trade Commission. 1992. *Potential Effects of a North American Free Trade Agreement on Apparel in CBERA Countries.* Washington, D.C.

Vobejda, Barbara. 1990. "Immigration Measure Raises Hopes, Worries." *Washington Post,* 4 November.

Wilkinson, Alec. 1989. "Big Sugar." *New Yorker,* 17 July.

Williams, Eric. 1970. *From Columbus to Castro: The History of the Caribbean, 1492–1969.* London: Andre Deutsch.

Wood, Charles. 1982. "Migration, Remittances, and Development: A Study of Caribbean Cane Cutters in Florida." Paper presented at the Latin American Studies Association Meeting, Washington, D.C., March.

World Bank. 1984. *World Development Report 1984.* New York: Oxford University Press.

Index

The Author

Ransford W. Palmer is professor of economics at Howard University. He received his Ph.D. from Clark University and his bachelor's and master's degrees from Marquette University. He is a past president of the Caribbean Studies Association, has served as chair of the Department of Economics at Howard University, and was an economics policy fellow at the Brookings Institution. He is the author of *The Jamaican Economy* (1968), *Caribbean Dependence on the United States Economy* (1978), *Problems of Development in Beautiful Countries: Perspectives on the Caribbean* (1984), and *In Search of a Better Life: Perspectives on Migration from the Caribbean* (1990).

The Editor

Thomas J. Archdeacon is professor of history at the University of Wisconsin-Madison, where he has been a member of the faculty since 1972. A native of New York City, he earned his doctorate from Columbia University under the direction of Richard B. Morris. His first book, *New York City, 1664–1710: Conquest and Change* (1976), examines relations between Dutch and English residents of that community during the late seventeenth and early eighteenth centuries. Building on that work, he has increasingly concentrated his research and teaching on topics related to immigration and ethnic-group relations. In 1983 he published *Becoming American: An Ethnic History.*

DATE DUE
